ALSO BY CHRISTOPHER HUDSON

The Final Act
The Killing Fields
Where the Rainbow Ends
Playing in the Sand
Colombo Heat

SPRING
STREET
SUMMER

SPRING STREET SUMMER

THE SEARCH FOR A LOST PARADISE

CHRISTOPHER HUDSON

ALFRED A. KNOPF   NEW YORK   1993

THIS IS A BORZOI BOOK
PUBLISHED BY ALFRED A. KNOPF, INC.

Library of Congress Cataloging-in-Publication Data

Hudson, Christopher.
Spring Street summer: the search for a lost paradise / by
Christopher Hudson.
p.   cm.
ISBN 0-394-58487-2
1. Hudson, Christopher—Homes and haunts—California—
Santa Cruz. 2. Santa Cruz (Calif.)—Social life and customs.
3. Novelists, English—20th century—biography.   I. Title.
PR6058.U313Z475   1993
828'.91403—DC20
[B]   93-6617
                            CIP

Manufactured in the United States of America
FIRST AMERICAN EDITION

For P.
and for my friends who were
in the house that summer

To understand oneself is the classic form of consolation; to elude oneself is the romantic.

—GEORGE SANTAYANA

ACKNOWLEDGEMENTS

I could not have written this book without the help and encouragement of Laura and the people who were living in Topside in the summer of 1976. Although my project represented an inevitable intrusion into their own lives, they showed unfailing courtesy and patience in answering my questions and taking the time to cast their minds back to a period which they did not all remember with equal pleasure. In dedicating this book to them, I feel I have repaid a small part of what I owe them.

Writing about UCSC I was lucky enough to be able to draw upon Ronald Saufley's unpublished monograph on the history of Oakes College – incidentally, the best short study of the University of California, Santa Cruz, that I've come across. I owe a debt of gratitude also, for their advice and hospitality, to Stuart and Harriett Cooper, to Ed McDermott and to his brother Joe (a Sherlock Holmes among Chinese scholars), to Robert Durling at Berkeley and Nelson Hilton at the University of Georgia, and to Shirley Letwin and David Grene without whose help many years ago this story would have been very different.

It would not have been told at all without the forbearance and understanding of my wife Kirsty McLeod, or the encouragement of Gill Coleridge, my literary agent, or the support of my two publishers, Fanny Blake at Penguin and Chuck Elliott at Knopf, both of whom read the MS in different drafts and gave me valuable advice. My thanks go to them, and also to Richard Cohen and Richard Luckett, who read the finished manuscript and made useful suggestions.

I have used Jacob Zeitlin's translation for the quotation from Petrarch's *De Vita Solitaria* on p. 109; the English Dominican translation, ed. A. C. Pegis, for the passages from Aquinas's *Summa Theologica* on p. 108 and *Summa Contra Gentiles* on p. 189; the Dorothy L. Sayers translation for the lines from Canto 30 of Dante's *Purgatorio* on p. 122 and from the final Canto of the *Paradiso* on p. 189; the *Bible Designed to be Read as Literature* for the lines from the Song of Solomon on p. 123; Robert Fitzgerald's translation of the *Æneid* for the lines from the Sixth Book on p. 125; G. D. H. Cole's translation for the quotation on p. 162 for Book Two of Rousseau's *Discourse on Inequality*; the James Strachey translation of Freud's *Beyond the Pleasure-Principle* for the quotations on p. 186; Jowett's edition of Plato for the passage from the *Timaeus* on p. 188; and C. K. Scott-Moncrieff's translation of Proust's *Remembrance of Things Past* for the passage from the end of *Swann's Way* on p. 249.

The quotations from Tom Stoppard's play *Travesties* on p. 225 and from T. S. Eliot's *Four Quartets* on p. 245 are reproduced by permission of Faber & Faber.

1

Rain was falling. That was the first adjustment I had to make. I remembered so much about that summer, and I didn't remember rain. But the heavens opened just as I turned off Route 101 through Castroville, The Artichoke Center Of The World. It fell in bolts, smashing against the glass of The Giant Artichoke (with its takeaway offers of Artichoke Loaf, French Fried Artichoke or a bag of Artichoke Batter Mix) and cascading down the sides of the monster green artichoke outside its front door, and whipping at the Artichoke Festival banner strung across Main Street. A few Castroville pedestrians were skedaddling for cover under artichoke-shaped umbrellas, and on the radio it was raining, raining in my heart, to the beat of the windscreen wipers on my rented Ford saloon.

I had flown all the way out here, to California, to find a missing person. His name . . . let's call him C. At the time I knew him, the mid-1970s, he was in his middle or late twenties – light brown hair, blue eyes, medium height and build, rather reserved . . . English as a matter of fact. He was travelling in the United States courtesy of an award scheme called the Harkness Fellowships, to whom he had sold the idea of researching concepts of Paradise in Western thought.

What was interesting about him, at least to me, was that he represented a typical Englishman, of the kind who get noticed more when they're abroad because they set themselves at an angle to everybody else. C. was casually

3

good-natured, with a rather dry sense of humour and a diffidence which could easily be mistaken for arrogance. He was charming, articulate and well-mannered. That was the problem, for some people. His manners made it almost impossible to discover what, if anything, was going on underneath. Asked *why* he'd come out there to write about Paradise, of all subjects, he'd laugh, with an air of faint embarrassment, and say, 'Well it seemed like a good idea at the time.'

But the point is this. C. underwent a metamorphosis. I don't think that's too strong a word to use. In the five or six months he was on the West Coast his reserve fell away. Out of the hard English chrysalis emerged something bright and vulnerable. It surprised everybody, this awkward, rather touching transformation – as though C. had escaped the ordinary world into one of those paradise gardens, the kind for which medieval painters saved their richest gold leaf and lapis-lazuli blue.

It happened in Santa Cruz. After seven months spent studying with the Committee on Social Thought at the University of Chicago, C. had decided to move on to some place more fitting to his Paradise theme. Here's where he ended up. Attaching himself to UCSC, the University of California, Santa Cruz, so that he could use the research facilities, he found lodging just down the hillside in a spacious white-painted redwood house at the end of Spring Street. Sharing the house with him were seven other people, all but one of them teachers or students at UCSC. There was also a girl he met, called Laura, who came by.

In this house, called Topside, above Santa Cruz, C. spent five spring and summer months. You might suppose that this experience in itself would have been enough to turn an

Old World stick into a New World sapling. Couldn't it have been simply a case of the chemical interaction of youth and sunlight – that joyful time of everything mattering enormously for the moment it happens and not an instant longer . . . when love is as easy as diving into a swimming-pool, and life is heart-breakingly carefree, solemn, meaningful and vivid?

I knew there was more to it than that. C. was no adolescent. He'd been a successful publisher and journalist; he'd just written his first book. He'd had girlfriends – 'as if it's any of your business' – and his fair share of things which couldn't be put right. Perhaps it was studying Paradise which changed him. Hard to know, since he'd never written any of it up for publication. In any event, it mattered that I should get to the heart of this, find out what happened and why. C. and I have a lot in common: at least I thought we had.

My aim was to use that white house above Santa Cruz as a starting-point. Spring Street was where it all happened. That was where I would begin – where the road ended in steep meadow, and a narrow drive led off on the right to Topside. I couldn't know what I would find. Maybe it hadn't all been as wonderful as I supposed it to have been . . . a whole lot of stuff going on which I never knew or never understood – jealousy, unhappy childhoods, the shadow of violence, even of violent death. I had to find out. I had to start somewhere. I was starting now.

The rain stopped as I drove through Soquel and down towards Santa Cruz on Route 1. Tumultuous swags of purple cloud painted the sky like a baroque Italian ceiling.

Either side of the highway the grass banks were carpeted in purple and yellow flowers. They glistened in the vivid, fading light. Already the dense blue of the Pacific was leaching away into the silvery-blue pallor that at twilight is like no other colour on earth. Dizzy after the long drive, I came off the ramp into a town which greeted me as a stranger, after thirteen years out of touch on the other side of the world. Sodium lights beckoned me down avenues that hadn't been built, to street corners I did not recognize. *No Vacancy* pulsed the neon banners above the baby swimming-pools.

At last I found a room on Ocean Street, a strip of fast-food franchises and cheap motels that cater for transients cruising off the freeway. The room smelt sweetly of urine. On the TV a balding man with cuff-links that caught the light introduced comic out-takes from his porno movie.

*   *   *

I'd flown over, tourist class, no problem, London to Los Angeles. In 1976 C. had arrived in Santa Cruz the travellers' way, by road. He'd set out from the Windy City on a bright clear April morning. *If you leave me now*, Chicago was chanting. *Ooh no, baby, plee-ase don't go.* But he couldn't stop, he had to keep going, he'd been on the run since England.

Tidying his life away into a cuttings-file, C. had got his girlfriend to drive him down from London to the Southampton docks. There, he'd walked up a gangplank and sailed off to the New World in a Cunard liner, with Captain Hehir on the bridge, Eric Mason leading the jogging round the Boat Deck and Albert Tinkler tickling the ivories in the Theatre Bar. In England he had lost his way. Arriving in New York he filled in a great many forms and caught the Amtrak to Chicago.

The mid-1970s . . . the pre-Aids time which John Updike's 'Rabbit' Angstrom, in common with a lot of Americans, thinks of as a Paradise Lost . . . when cocaine was still a prerogative of the middle classes, and the Santa Cruz Sheriff's Department hadn't run out of space in the County Jail; when Ollie North and Ivan Boesky hadn't embarked on the enterprises which were to turn them into household names; when the killing of a single Arab girl by Israeli troops on the West Bank still made the front page of *The New York Times*. Coming from the little walled garden of England into the vast dynamo of the United States, it took C. a long time to appreciate what people kept telling him – that there was a mood of jadedness around, even of fatigue, of the kind which comes after a long battle. The Vietnam War was over – and with it, the protests, the political strife, the nightly stress of the television news. There were no more body-bags to come home. It was a time for some peace and quiet and looking-inwards.

That suited C. just fine. Out here, he was determined to hold fast to Reason: as the means of rediscovering some kind of faith, in himself and in the world around him. Christians who experience a crisis of faith go on Retreat. C.'s idea of a Retreat was to tread the cloistered paths of a two-year university graduate programme. He didn't want to start analysing *why* he'd picked on Paradise as his field of study; it was better that he should rationalize the subject itself, get to grips with the facts of what people believed about it. That meant getting his terms of reference straight. He wasn't interested in the myths of Paradise: the utopian dreams of wishful-thinkers, the nostalgic Arcadias of poets and novelists, film-makers, landscape designers. He wanted to find something indissoluble: a sub-stratum of rock in which was embedded the essential truth about what made people yearn for a place they would never possess.

For C.'s purposes – holding fast to Reason – he couldn't have chosen better than Chicago. Chicago, above most American universities, was Reason made manifest. Steeped in the tradition of the Great Books of the Western World it cast a sceptical eye on whatever could not be deduced by empirical method. On the graduate programme of the Committee on Social Thought, prop. Saul Bellow, the intellectual ambience was as brisk as the wind which blew off Lake Michigan down the Midway. A colleague who roomed next door to him on Kimbark was writing a doctoral thesis on the psychology of narcissism. Somebody else on the programme was making an in-depth study of the Fool in *King Lear*. This was the kind of asylum C. had been looking for.

In the New Year of 1976 he moved off the University of Chicago campus to share a beautiful brownstone mansion on the near North Side of the city with a mournful millionaire whose name was Chuck. Large, paunchy and myopic, with thinning hair, Chuck was aged about twenty-six, at a rough guess. C. had met him through friends, and in one of his unpredictable flashes of generosity Chuck had offered him lodging, on condition that C. would look after the place at weekends when he jetted south to visit a girlfriend in Houston, Texas.

The mansion was magnificent in its late-Victorian opulence. It was like the town-house of a nineteenth-century steel magnate in the north of England – oak panelling, stained glass, tasselled lampshades, asparagus ferns, a tiger-skin, heavy velveteened furniture and Turkish carpets – C. felt like Oliver Twist in the house of Mr Brownlow. Everything was in period, including the iron bath C. used, on lion's-paw feet, big enough to hold an entire family.

Sadly, Chuck didn't have a family. He was looking for himself – had been looking for himself ever since his parents died seven years before and left him a fortune – and he seemed resigned to a long search. It took C. a while to appreciate his problem. In England it is relatively easy to deal with inherited wealth; the social Season was invented to help dispose of it in pleasurable ways. In the United States the work ethic is more ingrained at every level of society; a stigma attaches to the playboy figure. Chuck had tried to duck it by becoming an artist. An artist-photographer.

He took his work very seriously. His idols were Paul Strand and Harry Callahan, and his own pictures imitated their deceptively casual ordinariness. But whereas in *their* black-and-white street scenes and beach scenes ordinariness is charged with melancholy or menace, Chuck's photographs of lamp-posts and whitewashed walls remained, modestly, lamp-posts and walls. The Vision Thing (in the words of another rich man who had a better idea where he was going) was missing. Some part of Chuck knew this; it accounted for his moods of depression.

Nevertheless he was a kindly man. Not long after C. arrived, Chuck offered him cocaine, before breakfast. C. turned it down and poured the cornflakes. It was safer not to try any extract of narcotic shrub at Chuck's place. He had told C. the story of how in a small stoppered Chinese vase on the drawing-room mantelpiece he had kept his brother's ashes ('I didn't have anything else to remember him by, not even a *photograph*'). Next to the vase Chuck had a tin of grass and one night, shortly before C. arrived, his brother was accidentally smoked during a pot party. The vandal, when he'd stopped laughing, had promised to steal ashes from his mother's urn as a replacement. Whether or not she ended up on Chuck's mantelpiece, C. never found out.

It was a strange time. Outside the heavy red damask curtains snow was piling up and drivers were butting, Chicago-style, to get a parking space. People were falling dead in the streets, occasionally of their own accord. Inside, in the flock-papered dining-room, Chuck's dinner guests were looking bemusedly at his new English house-guest. After the usual discussion of the best resorts for powder snow, and the amusing gifts they had exchanged at Christmas a fortnight earlier, conversation had turned to analysts, and the analysts of analysts. After a while C. remarked lightly on the fact that he appeared to be the only person in the room who was not going to a shrink – indeed, had never been to one.

Silence.

Somebody inquired, 'How do you feel about that?'

Southside, on the University of Chicago campus, the wind blew ice off Lake Michigan and rattled branches of the few remaining trees which had not been cut down a year earlier in order to deter rapists. There was no notable violence on campus that winter but the smell of it hung in the air like a distant pall of smoke. C. took a British documentary film director and his recce team to a Southside jazz club for an evening of better blues-playing than any he was to hear subsequently in New Orleans. His party – three men and two women – were the only white people in the club. Around midnight the genial emcee's jokes about honkies started getting personal. C. paid the bill and departed. To listen to mid-Northside's reactions at the weekend's neighbourhood street-party (trestle-tables laden with vats of hot spaghetti bolognese steaming in the snowy air) he might have just come back from the wrong side of the 40th Parallel during the Tet offensive. None of the people around him had ever been that far south and unlocked the door of the car.

C. made some good friends in Chicago, including a woman lawyer who was generous as well as beautiful. I'm not sure, now, that I understand why he determined to move on elsewhere, except that he was having trouble pinning Paradise down, it kept slipping through his fingers, numbed by the wind-chill off the lake. He went to see the anthropologist Stephen Toulmin, then attached to the Committee on Social Thought, and asked him which one out of all the university campuses in the United States most closely approximated to the Garden of Eden.

It was mid-March. Stephen Toulmin put on his overcoat and went out to take soundings from some of the other Committee members (at the University of Chicago the most seemingly frivolous question is deemed worthy of serious thought). He returned with news of a unanimous decision. C. would find the earthly paradise, or its nearest equivalent, at the University of Santa Cruz on the coast of California.

The oracle had spoken. In early April C. threw his books and papers into the back of a green Ford Maverick which had seen better days, and headed westwards. By lunchtime he was well into Wisconsin cow country: white clapboard; green roofs; barns painted the colour of redcurrants with arched roofs that swept up to a point. Lunchtime, C. stopped off at a Dog n' Suds in Readstown for a Texasburger and home-made apple pie (under a shield announcing a Dog n' Suds award to Brent and Marlene Larson for Cleanliness of Facilities and Courtesy of Service and Quality of Food) and studied the map.

This was an America he had never seen and never expected to see except in old black-and-white movies like *It's a Wonderful Life*. It consisted of rolling plains on which small towns had been set down with the simplicity of stitching on a young girl's sampler: the main street, the church on a slight hill, the fine foursquare hotel. C. breakfasted in one of them the following morning, on the borders of Minnesota and South Dakota. The waitress wrote carefully in longhand on his bill *Have a good day. Tilla.*

On impulse, he turned off Interstate 90 in South Dakota, just before the Missouri River, on a road marked to Shelby in the Crow Creek Indian Reservation, once part of the 35,000-square-mile Great Sioux Reservation established after the Teton Sioux tribes surrendered to the US government exactly one hundred years ago. 'Shelby' turned out to consist of a gas station and some corrugated-iron shacks built in a square, the only evidence of collective living. Further down the dirt road were more scattered buildings, all of them dilapidated and run-down except the schoolhouse. A dead cow lay beside a wire fence on which a torn black scarf marched in the wind. In backyards and patches of meadow lay brightly coloured artefacts of modern technology – pumps, washing machines, tractor parts – cannibalized and left to rust. Nearby grazed the Indians' horses . . . sleek, well-cared-for, beautiful. Waiting for the past.

C. drove on towards Rapid City. At six-thirty he left the

highway and entered a silent, utterly deserted landscape. Stopping the car he got out and walked up to an overlook. At his feet, astonishingly, lay an entire mountain kingdom. An immensity of peaks and crevasses, valleys and buttes, stretched to the horizon in strange, dry, eroded, buff-coloured shapes flecked with pink by the late afternoon sky.

For half an hour he walked in the Badlands among massive rock formations, inspiring and mountainous yet none of them higher than a multi-storey car park. The sun was sinking. The earth was grey and cracked like elephants' feet. Nothing moved. No birds sang. An enormous hush had fallen. Across the valley it grew suddenly dark. The sky vanished in sheets and bolts of lightning. Moistness on the sudden breeze carried with it the sweetish smell of juniper: the smell of the Mediterranean, of sunburned hills plunging into blue sea . . . the smell of where he was going to. As he returned to the car the storm broke, overhead, and flash-lit the jagged peaks and ridges in the electric darkness.

C., whether he knew it or not, had left the East behind. He drove on through the Black Hills, and Wyoming, and over the Loveland Pass in the Colorado Rockies, and down into Mormon country. Detouring along the Dirty Devil River it was like the Badlands all over again, except to scale this time, and mile after mile of it. The earth yellowish, supporting nothing except a few dull clumps of sagebrush: it felt like the wilderness before the promised land. Nevada was more of the same: the vast dry brown seabed of the extinct inland sea, sagebrush, juniper, near-deserted roads and sometimes in the distance, across the empty table-land, a vision of white mountains, their peaks obscured by cloud and thickening dusk.

On Main Street, Eureka, he went past what looked like a genuine early-Frontier saloon, with a crumbling wooden balcony propped above an old drugstore window. Engraved in the brick above the balcony – THE MOVIES. Film-set scenery: it couldn't be far now. Austin, Fallon, and the mountains began to fall away; Sparks, Reno, then up into the pine forests of the Sierras.

Somewhere after that, he turned off the Interstate and came down out of winter and a desert landscape into a valley of overhanging green filled with dog violets and yellow poppies and the smell of moist earth. Sunlight struck the green leaves of the maples and turned them into living tissue, setting the chlorophyll working and the sap rising as on the third day of Creation. Tuning to Sacramento he lighted on Elton John –

> *And I think it's gonna be a long, long time*
> *Till touch down brings me round again to find*
> *I'm not the man they think I am at home, Oh no, no, no*

Singing, he drove down into California, and spring.

In San Francisco he picked up a phone and dialled a Santa Cruz number. The number (*c/o Andrea*) had been scribbled down for him in Chicago, seven days and three thousand miles ago, by a friend of Stephen Toulmin's called Terry Hoffman whose face C. had already forgotten.

A deep male voice answered the phone. 'You want Andrea?'

'Andrea, yes. It says here Terry's a friend of hers.'

'No kidding. She's in darkest Africa. You want me to leave a message?'

C. muttered something apologetic about the suggestion of a bed for the night, before he started looking for a room to rent.

'You from England?'

'Um, yes.'

'That's probably all right. Andrea won't mind if you crash out here for a couple of days. Unless she comes back early . . .'

C. arrived in Santa Cruz that night on the coast road. People he stopped to ask the way to Spring Street all raised their arms and pointed up, as if it were some kind of celestial destination they were heading him towards. Leaving the city centre he drove past porch lamps illuminating half-moons of green lawn, past snatches of music and voices round a late-night barbecue, higher and higher, until the lights of the town stretched out below and C. came to the last street heading upwards and at the end of that, round the back of a big brick farmhouse, the drive which led to Topside, the last house on the hill.

He rang the bell. It was answered straight away by a pretty, snub-nosed girl with bright, sad eyes. She was wearing a blue night-shirt. Her feet were bare. When she saw him she widened her eyes and gave a little bounce on the balls of her feet.

'Hi. You the guy who called, right? I'm Hélène, hi. Howard told us you were coming, but I think the others have gone to bed. You're sleeping in Andrea's room, right? Have you really been on the road since Chicago? I'll show you the room. It's really neat. Then you can bring your stuff, okay?'

There was a divan bed at one end of Andrea's room, in a kind of sunroom annexe. C. brought a bag out of the car, washed, and lay down to sleep. He felt drowsy and contented, like a wanderer who'd come home. Or else it was something in the night air through the open windows, as if he was breathing a distillation of the music and the sweet smells of flowering bushes in the gardens below. In the vaulting night, stars wavered towards him like the beams of all the cars that had headed his way on the long journey west . . .

He woke early and found himself floating in the clouds and went to sleep again. The second time he opened his eyes, the sun slanting in through the tremendous panes of glass had burned the mist away. What he saw, as he went to the window, was something which every subsequent prospect, from the garden, from the sun-terrace, from the living-room, would never be able to repeat on the same scale.

Beneath him were descending balconies of pink and white roses, bounded on either side by arroyos which plunged down the hillside in a dark-green ambuscade of fern, bramble and holm-oak. Above the narrow canyon on the right-hand side, a wooded spur of land, curving inward, half-enclosed the garden and protected it from the west wind off the ocean. In the distance, a long way below, the toy roofs and buildings of Santa Cruz shone as pinkly as in a Tuscan landscape out to the horizon, except in one corner of the picture where, for the sake of balance and perspective, a crescent of pale blue ocean was painted in.

Inside, tasselled and beaded leather cushions lay heaped against the corners of the sun-room. On the walls of the living area hung bright East African tapestries, bark paintings, grinning masks, and a couple of beautiful Nigerian heads, high-cheekboned with smooth-lidded empty eyes, sculpted out of a dark hardwood. Neatly shelved on either side of the work-table were books of social anthropology marked with scholarly pink and yellow paper tabs.

The room vibrated with Andrea's presence like the skin of a drum. C. wished that he could have got to know Andrea. Or any of the others who lived in this white house above the clouds. He decided to take up Howard's suggestion and stay a second night. And then a third, and a fourth . . .

This house was where C. stayed to do his research into Paradise. People have asked me what was remarkable about the summer in Spring Street that it should have changed C. so much. If I knew, I wouldn't have needed to make this journey now. But usually I tell them this story. It probably doesn't mean much, but it always seemed to C. to sum up the craziness of that time.

It was a Sunday afternoon in late May. A soft-blowing breeze carried sweet smells from the rose-bushes. The bougainvillea was in flower, and the beautiful red camellia up against the kitchen wall. A humming-bird flickered in the lemon tree. C., wearing nothing but a pair of rather grubby long trousers, was kneeling in the vegetable garden down behind Howard's annexe, learning how to plant squash in neat rows. Working beside him were three girls who roomed with him at Topside. Their names were Lowrie, Jan and Hélène – all young and very pretty students at UCSC. The sun was hot, and the girls had taken off all their clothes. Silently and seriously Adam and three Eves scooped up the friable earth, as dry and fragrant as tobacco-dust, into small soft mounds and pushed seedlings into them, pretending for a blissful hour that supermarkets selling packaged squash hadn't been invented, and that this was the morning of the world.

Out of the trees and wild undergrowth at the edge of the tilled soil crawled a snake. It was brown and plump, about four feet long. It flickered its tongue.

The Paradise scholar, terrified, shouted a warning. He knew what was supposed to happen next. The girls looked round and stood up, dusting the earth off their legs.

'It's only a gopher snake, it's not poisonous,' declared Lowrie the biology student. She picked it up and let it glide between her breasts, over her shoulder and down her back. Hélène and Jan hurried over to her with cries of delight. C. stood with his mouth open, rooted to the spot.

'Hey this is *fun*,' cried Hélène, lifting the snake off Lowrie and draping it round her neck. Jan came up and they passed the creature from hand to hand, its dry scales rippling over their bare brown bodies.

'Wow! Shall we keep it? What shall we call it?'

C. stared at them, speechless. His brain whirled with paradigms. Innocence and beauty playing with the serpent – what could it mean? All he vaguely realized was that a divine joke was being played on him. He had made his way to the West Coast to find a place corresponding to the Garden of Eden. Now God was providing the *dramatis personae*.

The Englishman took his turn with the snake. It slid around him with unhurried deliberation, its mind set on lower things. Then it crawled away into the trees. The sun was still shining. The breeze still blew. The girls had bent back to their gardening. But C. knew that something irreversible had occurred. Whatever higher power had set the scene was now writing the script.

By this time C. had pretty much got used to the zaniness all around him. They'd found a bed for him in a wide alcove at the foot of the stairs, and although it was more public than he was used to, nobody seemed to mind, so why should he?

Nobody seemed to mind about anything much – except for health and hygiene. There was No Smoking at Topside: the women insisted on that. Otherwise, nature was left to take its course. About a week after he arrived, Jan slipped into C.'s bed in the alcove with a casualness which appalled him. She didn't say very much. As a biology student she was naturally curious about all new species, Englishmen included. Although C., taken by surprise, did not respond with the dedication her research deserved, she conceived a tenderness for him which lasted until a rival came on the scene and took over the case-study.

It seemed intolerably narcissistic to C. at first, this lack of moral restraint, as though the inhabitants of Topside were a throwback to Rousseau's noble savages, untutored in the ways of civilization, making up the rules as they went along. There were house rules, to be sure. Housework was on a rota, to be carried out between Saturday morning and Sunday night. Cleaning the Fridges; Emptying the Dustbins; Collecting for the Phone Bill – and heaven help the person who forgot or who was too freaked out to get it together. Howard the landlord, heavy-shouldered, flashing-eyed, black-bearded, beetle-browed, would prowl through the house and issue loud threats of expulsion to the offender.

But the sun was too warm, and the grass too soft, and the aspect too beautiful, for hard feelings. The house encouraged inhibitions to fall away. C. wrote to his girlfriend in London – '*I'm writing this letter in a chair on a semi-circular balcony in front of a low stone wall covered in lush green creeper. Beyond, the ground falls away down a garden hillside of flowering trees and shrubs, towards a small canyon filled with maple and young redwood, and beyond them to a panoramic view of the town of Santa Cruz and the Pacific. It's still quite early in the morning, so the ocean is hidden in a whitish haze, but already the sun is high and warm, the birds are singing, and a light breeze chimes the cowbell on a fence post. It's a very languorous, luxurious life ...'*

C., as I remember, at first responded by becoming a parody of himself. He strode around the house wearing long trousers and an ironic smile, as if to distance himself from the sensuousness on every side. The others, I think, felt tolerantly that an English writer would present a charming addition to the menagerie at Topside. C. took the attitude that the others were the menagerie and he was looking in at them through the bars.

One other person in the household probably shared this attitude, and that was Katie, Howard's eleven-year-old daughter. Most of her formative years she had spent with her mother at hippie schools, which made her, more literally than any of them, a child of the sixties, educated in peace, love, harmony and organic foods. Her mother had taught at one of these places: a Montessori school called Daybreak, set up by Joan Baez. She had majored in anthropology, Katie's mother, and she used to teach Katie and the other kids Indian rituals, and take them to see wild-dog dances in Arizona ... but then, sometime before C. arrived, her mother had gone off to do her own thing, nobody seemed to know where.

Katie had come back to Topside to live with her father. Since there wasn't room for her in the annexe she camped out in the dining-room of the main house, sleeping on a mattress, with her few toys and possessions arranged neatly round it. Communing with nature hadn't given Katie much grasp of how to read and write. Howard, unimpressed by progressive education, arranged for his daughter to go to a proper, public school in Santa Cruz.

C. was mightily amused by the idea of this eleven-year-old who had renounced her early life as a drop-out and was now heavily into the three Rs. A quick learner, she naturally was way behind other children of her age, so it turned out that there weren't too many meals in the dining-room that summer in Spring Street. Katie was doing her homework.

It was Lowrie, Howard's former girlfriend, who had more or less adopted Katie by the time C. arrived, helping her with her schoolwork and making sure that she had enough to eat and wear. Younger than C. – her graduation from UCSC was coming up that summer – Lowrie was one of those responsible, serious-minded girls who are indistinguishable from the mature women they will become. She had greenish eyes and curly brown hair, and a face which with a modicum of vivacity could have been beautiful. She had taken upon herself a matronly burden of responsibility for the Spring Street household, energetically washing, dusting and gardening, before joining the others in the sun.

Then, one day in early summer, coming back from the University library, C. noticed that Lowrie had been dislodged from her pole position under the lemon tree in the yard. Howard had moved another girl into his life, a blonde half-Hawaiian beauty named Rose. At first, nothing much seemed to change. Lowrie went on busily gardening and tidying, with perhaps a sharper look of determination on her face.

Another week went by, and C. happened upon Lowrie,

wearing not a stitch of clothing, sweeping the patio outside the back door and setting up a deckchair. She had moved into the spare bedroom, off the downstairs passage, along from his alcove.

From now on, her biology exams finished, Lowrie would spend much of the day stark naked, busying herself around the house. I don't think it ever occurred to C. at the time that it was a silent but deliberate weapon against Rose in their rivalry over Howard. To him it seemed entirely in keeping with her practical nature. The late spring and summer in Santa Cruz were as hot and almost as dry that year as they were in Britain. Nevertheless, encountering this brown, slim, attractive figure sunbathing on the patio or gardening beneath the stone balcony as C. carried his typewriter-table out into the orchard, it was some time before he could muster up 'Hi, Lowrie! How's it going?' in a decently casual tone of voice.

The ploy was unsuccessful. Howard had eyes only for Rose. Although she was one of his students, like Lowrie and Jan, there was nothing at all homely about Rose. Her naturalness was of a different order. Tanned a milky gold, wonderfully sensuous, she inhabited a world of incipient sophistication, in which men were Men and women were Women.

That completed Howard's side of the household. A similar nexus existed on the far side of the house from Howard, around the person of Andrea, blonde and tigerish Andrea, C.'s contact and good friend. Whenever C. used to talk about Topside, it was first of her suite of rooms, and not only because that's where he slept for the initial few nights in Spring Street.

When Andrea was back from her African travels, he'd

join a group of them, late at night, sitting in rattan basket chairs round the barrel-table which she had bought from the Drug Rehabilitation Center in Santa Cruz. Andrea would have lit candles, and the light would flicker on her African rugs and the fabrics on the walls, and on the ebony Makondi masks and the ebony man with a cloven hoof, grinning from ear to ear. C. would have brought some wine, and Andrea would hold the floor with fantastical tales of Monarch butterfly migrations, and being tailed by the FBI, and the times she'd spent with an Australian coalminer, a blues musician, various political radicals and a world-famous natural scientist with whom she'd sat on the edge of the Bay barking at seals until five in the morning.

Andrea's rooms were always full of music – classical, jazz or blues – and every now and then she would play the flute to them (she'd studied flute in Chicago) and one of the cats – perhaps Rafiki the Abyssinian, not so much a cat as a space creature with huge eyes which never blinked but just gazed – would get up on the table in a kind of trance and wind itself round her shoulders.

Jan was as radical as anybody C. came across in Santa Cruz. If she'd been around a few years earlier, she'd have joined the Weathermen. She had causes and goals about which she was passionately single-minded. That summer (inspired by Andrea and her anthropological research) it was the impoverished sharecroppers in the San Joaquin Valley, eastwards over the Santa Cruz Mountains. Jan spent her spare time campaigning to improve their lot and organizing bus rides to do fieldwork and learn about artesian wells. C. joined one of these rides, along with a dozen of Jan's colleagues carrying clipboards and shoulder-bags, their faces grave with the significance of making a foray against the oppressive forces of capitalism. They stopped on the way at a health-food shop to buy raisin bread and nuts for lunch. The sharecroppers were bemused: but the gesture had been made, and the little group was back in time for tea.

When Andrea cut her hair short, Jan cut her hair short. So did Helen, who had Europeanized her name to Hélène because she was studying French and Comparative Literature. Hélène lived downstairs in the room behind Jan – a box-room hardly bigger than the battered little Mazda RX which she parked in the drive. She was seeing an extra-ordinary creature called Boris, a dapper little man who wore a yellow waistcoat and claimed to be a Russian pianist. C. liked Hélène and felt protective towards her. She was everybody's younger sister – childlike, puppyish, affection-ate, demanding. Like something newly born she had no armour against life; everything had a capacity to hurt or delight her. She would sit with C. and talk for hours on the sun-terrace about love and history and the idea of culture in Europe and fluorocarbons depleting the ozone layer . . .

Actually it is my impression that everybody in that household got on pretty well, with the forgivable exception of Lowrie and Rose. They all met up over a drink in the kitchen. They all did their rota of house duties without complaint. They worked in the garden, three or four at a time. The only person who kept himself slightly aloof was Rick, a sad-eyed Midwesterner who taught Chinese Politics up the hill. He lived next to Andrea in a big front room with its own bathroom. It was as uncommunicative as Rick himself – a desk made out of a door-top, an inflatable bed like an air mattress on the floor, a few shelves made out of crates, a couple of chairs and a cupboard. He played a lot of folk music in his room, and the rest of the house wouldn't see him for days at a stretch. Then he would drive up in his big six-cylinder blue-and-white Dodge van with an unfamiliar girlfriend whom he would formally introduce before disappearing again.

The one place Rick could quite often be seen was in the garden. Rick believed in communal labour. For his doctorate, he was participating in a study of a model Maoist community in China, an ideal village where production was supposedly increased by hard work free of any modern technology. So on a warm Sunday afternoon there would be Rick, dressed in a Mao jacket and blue Mao cap with a red star, hoeing in the vegetable garden. Unfortunately, because of the dry weather, the ground was hard, and Rick, together with his cadre of Jan and Hélène, had determined to harvest brussels sprouts. So the hoe was put aside and Rick rented a roto-tiller. Even then, he did not abandon his principles. He got Jan to work the roto-tiller while he trod in her wake, picking the stones out of the turned soil.

Rick could be friendly, even charming. C. would talk to him about Chicago where (like Andrea) he came from, or about Reagan vying with Carter for the Presidency while good old Gerald Ford, campaigning in Texas, tried to eat the corn shucks round a hot tamale. Other times, Rick would be morose and enigmatic; days would go past when he'd avoid C.'s eye. But in due course Spring Street worked its magic on Rick, too.

Probably it happened when he slipped a disc in his back and was confined to the house for a couple of weeks. C. would come in to find a small horde of Chinese Politics students gathered in the living-room with Rick flat out on his back on the carpet, lecturing them, and the sun streaming in through the picture-window like a Bonnard painting. Towards the end of the summer, when C. returned to the house in an afternoon of humming-birds and bougainvillea, to find Rose stretched out naked on the grass under the lemon tree reading a book and Rick kneeling beside her rubbing sun-tan oil into her shoulders, he knew that the house had claimed possession of its most reluctant guest.

*   *   *

Yesterday's rain had left the air sharp and fresh with the smell of the sea. I checked out of the porno motel on Ocean Street and drove round Santa Cruz for a while to get my bearings. At the top of the town I turned right on Highland, shifted down a gear and drove up Spring Street. I noticed inconsequential things – a bird darting in and out of sweet-clover, a woman in pink trousers opening the doors of the gabled Lutheran church which stood on the corner. Intrusive new houses basked in suburban pools of grass and tarmac. Then – nothing. The street came to a dead end at a picket fence which held back tall meadow grasses. And on the right a narrow, untended drive, as straight as a plummet-line into the depths of memory. Beside it, the address picked out in tin buttons on a redwood slat:

700 Spring Street.

I turned up the drive. The car brushed the undergrowth on either side. Twigs snapped under the wheels. Then the house was there in front of my eyes, as suddenly as turning over a photograph. The long, white frontage under the slope of the tiled roof, the annexe off to the side where Howard had lived ... nothing had changed, nothing was out of place. I rang the bell. Nobody answered. I rang again. After a minute, I tried the door. It opened, as if I had been expected.

'Hallo? Is anybody home?'

The rounded English vowels dropped into silence. I advanced into the hall. Unopened letters in a wicker basket on the table. Ahead the door was open into the sunlit living-room, smaller than I remembered it, almost bare except for a white rug on the parquet floor, two wooden seats stacked against the wall beside a potted yucca plant, and a TV in the fireplace. Walking over to the picture-window I looked out over the plunging arroyos, over the roofs of Santa Cruz, to the still blue daub of Monterey Bay. Behind me the room filled with comfortable chairs, bookcases, the echo of remembered voices –

'There's no room for anyone else.'
'Hey, we've got space!'
'The alcove downstairs. There's a bed. He can use my cupboard . . .'
'It's got my files in. And he doesn't want to sleep down there –'
'So move the files, Rick!'

I turned back into the emptiness. It was unsettling, the absence of clues. The kitchen, where people had talked long into the night in a litter of beer cans and empty coffee cups, was emptily tidy too. Long gone the famous aquarium beside the back door where eleven-year-old Katie had fed the gaudy predator fish and scooped out the half-devoured remains of the ones that by some random evolutionary accident turned out to be their prey.

'You can tell they're dying when they look up to the sky.'
'Oh yes, Katie?'
'Fish go to heaven too, you know!'

Back through the hall and down the corridor to the suite of rooms at the end where C. had lived in state for his first two nights in Topside before moving downstairs. Again the door was ajar, the room empty. In place of beaded African masks and Andrea's beautiful, dying ginger cat stalking painfully among the tribal cushions, shelves of law books stood on bricks against the wall. On the bare floor, a pile of motorcycle magazines.

'Hallo? Anybody?'

No answer. No sound except the hollow tread of my footsteps on the wooden floors. People must be living here, but the ghosts in my head had more solidity, more possession of the place. I retraced my steps to the hall and turned down by the front of the house to a little wooden gate which led down stone steps to the orchard – as we had grandly called our three orange trees and one little grapefruit tree, *Citrus paradisi*, on their patch of grass bordered by flowering shrubs.

In the summer afternoons twelve years ago, C. had taken a folding table and chair and the typewriter to sit and work here, under the orange blossom. Of the orchard now there was a single tree left, standing forlornly in the overgrown grass. The point beyond, where C. used to walk with Laura in the fragrance of juniper and pine, halfway between the canyons and the evening sky, had been bulldozed into a red scar of earth and rubble.

Then I realized I was looking at the garden.

There was no garden. The wilderness had broken through. Weeds and creepers encroached in ugly profusion up the balconies which the first architects of Topside had built as a protection against the wild disorder below. Howard's rose-bushes had disappeared. Rank undergrowth choked the flowering oleander. Skunkweed overgrew the paved pathways beneath the sun-terrace. Thickets of fern and live-oak had crossed the old divide and marched up the hill almost to the walls of Topside; so that, from where I was standing, the house looked as if it was about to plunge into the dark canyons below.

I walked the top path, through the skunkweed and the brambles, to the far side of the house on the hill. The vegetable garden, where we had planted out squash in line abreast, had been obliterated under a rubbish tip sprouting wild nasturtiums. Only now was it possible to see that one small part of the garden hadn't changed. Below the brick path between the house and the annexe I came upon the square of green lawn with its lemon tree, and a bougainvillea bursting scarlet beside the wall. Under the lemon tree a plump girl in an orange swimsuit lay on her back sunbathing. She looked up at me, without surprise, and held her headphones away from her ears.

'Hi there. Were you looking for Phil?'

If I had needed proof that time had moved on, it lay before me in an orange swimsuit with headphone trim. It was futile – absurd! – this whole idea of mine that by coming back to where it happened I could somehow rerun the past, like an old video. I mumbled something. The girl clapped her headphones back on.

*

Looking back at the house, I started wondering. Even the most dispossessed of us cherish the memory of a golden age in our lives. It might be the last-ever family holiday on the beach, hunting for Viking treasure in the sand with parents who were still together and smiling in the scrapbook photographs. It might be a summer camp coming-of-age. A fishing trip. A honeymoon in a hotel in the Old Quarter with the smell of croissants rising deliciously as you opened the painted shutters to the morning sun.

Memory keeps this golden age locked away; fresh enough – or so the convenient illusion has it – that we don't ever need to go back. But the pictures we evoke in the mind develop a spurious, artificial charm which comes from the process of memory itself, as the mind's eye takes over from the senses. It is fear that stops us seeking out these pictures in reality; fear that the place we love to recall will have altered so much that it supplants our memory of how it used to be. So we go on remembering – more distantly, more mistily, more spuriously with every year that passes – until our golden age is no more than a token, a trinket on the mind's back shelf.

I suppose I'd had some notion that this house in Santa Cruz would have helped me find the missing person I was looking for – the Englishman who had discovered the meaning of happiness here and been transformed under its influence, yet had nevertheless decided to leave it behind. All I'd found so far was weeds and emptiness. But this didn't necessarily presuppose that I had succumbed to the illusion of a golden age. Just because the place had changed, and wilderness had entered in, didn't mean that the others wouldn't remember Topside the same way I did – and remember C. too. And there was something else. Or rather, somebody.

Laura. She had come here maybe ten times in all, but her presence pervaded the place.

Standing in the yard, I made my mind up. I would go looking for Howard and Katie, Andrea and Rick, Jan and Hélène and talk to them about that summer of 1976. Perhaps what they said would prove to me that I'd been imagining the whole experience. But if they happened to feel the same way, my journey would not have been wasted. We could renew this corner of Eden out of composite images, shared memories. An act of collective recall! Not to bring back the past exactly, but to conserve it against the acid rain of time. And I could solve some mysteries of my own.

I had to find them first. Thirteen years on they could be scattered across the world ... abroad ... dead. Jesus, I didn't even remember their surnames! Except Howard's. Howard Tellier was where I would start. He had been the landlord, the master of ceremonies. He had been the *gardener*. I turned back to the orange swimsuit under the lemon tree.

'May I please use your phone?'

＊   ＊   ＊

At seven o'clock the next morning I was studying a square of road-map between the pancake and the coffee in the Golden West Pancake House, before the journey up the coast highway to Oakland. Howard hadn't been a problem to trace. The last address I'd had for him, a decade ago, was at a university on the East Coast. Now, according to UCSC records, he was working as the Technical Manager of a Silicon Valley company somewhere in the Bay Area. I'd rung the company; Howard was out of his office; the switchboard patched me through to some subsidiary where he was on a 'field inspection'.

'Chris? Of course I remember. You still owe me that bottle of whisky.'

'Whisky?'

'That's right. After you swapped your horse's skull for that Indian bark painting you went away with.'

The voice, strong, deep, emphatic, brought the man foursquare in front of me, an imposing presence. I mumbled something.

'Hey, no sweat. We'd love to see you. Come for lunch tomorrow. Come and meet Tessa.'

Tessa?

I finished breakfast and set off up the Cabrillo Highway in the direction of Half Moon Bay. It was a day of light and dark shadows, and there was a white lacing of breakers on the turquoise shawl of the Pacific. Traffic was light. It had been a cold spring and the curving beaches were empty except for a few surfers in rubber wetsuits who squatted by their campers, polishing their surfboards. The sun they were waiting for came out as I drove through Half Moon Bay and headed north towards Pacifica and San Francisco, thinking about the man I was going to meet.

Tessa?

The way I remembered Howard, he was too independent ever to have settled into a steady relationship. Apart from the biochemistry he'd taught up on campus, Howard devoted himself to looking after the house and to pursuing women – but he was, first and foremost, a scientist. Beauty at its purest was to be found in form that was perfectly matched to its purpose. A canoe, or the cylinders of a motorbike, appealed more deeply to his sense of the aesthetic than would a roomful of Botticellis, which, because they appeared to serve no practical purpose, would have drawn from him a purely sentimental appreciation. Music moved him to tears; a perfectly tooled camshaft bearing filled him with exultation. Women came somewhere in between.

That's not to say that he didn't have unbounded admiration for the type of women – pretty, full-breasted, generous-hipped – who obviously matched the purpose of God's creation. The confusion arose when the woman turned out to view her identity in larger terms than might be applied to a canoe or an automobile engine. Not content with surging on Howard's king-sized waterbed, and cooking him loving meals in the annexe kitchen, she'd start clearing shelves and organizing space for herself. More clothes would arrive, spilling over into the wardrobe at the back of the garage, beside the door to the tiny kitchen. Ambitious plans would be laid for an asparagus bed in the vegetable garden.

As the signs of dependency appeared, so Howard would become strange and remote. He would spend more time in the main house, casting an eye over his daughter Katie's schoolwork or sitting in our kitchen holding forth to anybody who came along. Or else he would take one of the tiny brown MDA pills which he refined from mescaline in the University laboratories (so Spring Street rumour had it) and go out at night and lie naked in the grass, hugging the stars to his chest.

Sailing in on the summer breeze, San Francisco looked like an overgrown seaside town, its pastel-coloured chalets winding up the hill under a grey-blue sky. I crossed Bay Bridge on 80 and then bore right on Highway 24 and the Warren Freeway towards the Oakland Hills. Drawing in to a supermarket I bought the largest bottle of whisky I could find and looked around for something to take Tessa. Maybe Howard had pulled out of that phase, although I couldn't bring myself to believe it. What was he likely to make of me coming at him out of the past with a fusillade of questions about things he might not wish to remember? It had taken him a long time to lose his wariness of C. when he first arrived, the wariness of the landlord towards the stranger who turns up on his doorstep alone and late at night. At the house-meeting called on the second night to decide democratically whether C. should be allowed to stay, Howard had been stern. The house was full; a new arrival would alter the balance; he'd have to re-allocate everyone's responsibilities.

Howard was voted down. He gave in gracefully, and before long he had accepted C. as one more exhibit in his aquarium of exotics. It was the satisfying Englishness of his new tenant, I think, which appealed to him more than who he was or what he was doing. As a fragment of the Old World thrown up by chance in his backyard, C. possessed a kind of solidity, like one of the stable elements in the Periodic Table to whose balance of electrons all the more volatile elements aspire.

I was nervous about this meeting. Thirteen years is a long time. Perhaps Howard wouldn't recognize C. in the person he saw before him. I no longer regarded myself as a modest, vulnerable, sensitive visitor poking his head round the Golden Door. A decade of 1980s materialism had put paid to that frame of mind.

Whatever innocence there had been in the scholar of Paradise who had driven up to Topside that night with a telephone number in his hand had gone for good. I regarded myself as a hard-headed professional writer now, with schedules to follow and appointments to keep. I was enough of a success not to be too constantly reminded of failure. I had a family, a mortgage, an accountant, an agent, and a consciousness that time was money and the clock was ticking away. At least the past was timeless and secure, or so I supposed. That was all the common ground we were likely to need.

Higher and higher I drove up into the hills, the landscape showing signs of rugged independence up here above the Bay. Turning right, I came to an area of new housing carved out of the side of the hill ridge – detached two-storey homes with tiled roofs and beige stone, clapboard-faced walls, not unlike the new houses along Spring Street. Road signs were part of the sales pitch: Elysian Fields Drive proclaimed the first one I came to. It led down the ridge to a small enclave of houses nestling in a semi-circle where the road ended. The air was humming with sounds of motorized lawnmowers. A man washing his car with a shower-fitting attached to his hosepipe gave me a friendly wave.

Checking the address, I pulled up outside the nearest house on the right. It was identical to the others, except for the ploughed-up earth on the steep slope behind, ready to be reclaimed for planting out.

I rang the bell beside the door with its smart brass fittings. The man who answered it was a little shorter than me, clean-shaven, with a neat haircut and mild, intelligent eyes behind brown spectacles. Wrong number. I prepared to apologize and fumbled in my pocket for the address.

'Chris?'

I stared. He held out his hand.

'Come in. It's real nice to see you.'

The astonishment must have been written on my face. As Howard led me into the hall, past the baby-buggy, he slapped me on the back.

'Didn't recognize me, huh?'

'Well, for a moment –'

'It's been a long time. A lot of changes. You haven't met my wife Tessa. And Gregory!'

He introduced me to a woman who wasn't at all like the voluptuous creatures who had sunbathed under the lemon tree in Spring Street. Tessa was small and pale and slim, very slim, with a pretty face and straight blonde hair. Cradled in her arms was a dark-eyed little boy about a year old who put out a pudgy hand to grasp my gift of whisky. Howard grinned.

'You see, he's inherited my vices before he knows what to do with them. Come into the sitting-room. Everything looks new, because –'

'Because it *is* new!' laughed Tessa.

'We only moved in like three, four months ago, when I knew where I was going to be.' He led me into a sunny, white-walled room, open to the dining-room and kitchen area. A vase of bright blooms stood on the glass side-table. 'This whole area has been opened up to new housing just recently. It's real high on the ridge, with views down over the Bay and the Naval Base. I like to have space. Somewhere with a view, you know!'

He poured some white wine. I tried to reorient myself with the new certainties I saw all around: the successful executive with his young family in a smart new house with a view, pouring Mondavi for the weekend lunch guest. I'd expected ... but I should have known when I saw the double garage on the way in, with cacti in flowerpots outside and no tyres and spare parts lying around or oil stains on the concrete floor. The Noble Savage had put on a business suit and melted into the crowd. What was I doing, prompting his memories of a past he'd probably lost all interest in?

'That's a good car you've got,' he said. 'Hertz?'

'Avis.'

'The last time we talked I was still driving a motorcycle. I had a car, a black Sunbeam Alpine, but it was dead in the garage. Damn machine, I couldn't get it going. And you know what the problem was? I'd got the distributor from a London taxi.'

All this time he was scrutinizing me intently. 'So what's all this about?' he asked. 'You said something about writing a memoir about the people who were in Spring Street, and bringing in the stuff about Paradise?'

'Yes, that's —'

'Is that what you do now? You're a writer?'

'Mostly. And a journalist.'

'What have you written?'

'Novels, mostly.' This wasn't going the way I'd intended. 'What are you doing at the moment? You said something on the phone about going off to Korea tomorrow morning.'

'That's right. There's a conference. They want me to talk about innovation in micro-technology. I'm spending a bit of time in the Far East these days —'

'*A lot of time!*' This from Tessa in the kitchen.

'They keep having these international conferences. I don't get to London much, though. There's no really interesting front-line research going on in Europe right now.'

Howard was no longer teaching. Or dropping MDA, or lying out on the warm grass. He was Technical Manager at one of the most advanced micro-technology companies in the world, which made semi-conductor chips for the big computer firms. He was a high-flier, a hotshot, with seventy engineers working under him; he entertained delegations of Japanese scientists and attended international conferences. The rewards were great. So were the penalties for failing to innovate. This was a company which fired anybody who wasn't constantly ahead of the game. The in-house managers circled each other like blood-crazed sharks, looking for the first signs of burn-out. Howard was good. Howard was out in front. But, at forty-two, he was feeling the pressure. It could be that a board directorship would come his way. But in a matter of months – at most a couple of years – he'd either be up or out.

All this came out off-handedly. All Howard really wanted to talk about was Spring Street. He put his glass of wine down and went off to get the album of photographs, while his son wheeled a toy lawnmower backwards and forwards, solemnly cutting the carpet.

'Here. Look at this. The only way you can see the whole house, the lane and all, looking across the pastures from above. I guess the old Captain, when he was looking for a place to build a house in the 1930s, talked some farmer out of his worthless piece of pasture there, with arroyos heading over the cliff below.'

'There were horses –'

'Sure. Down by the driveway, in what was once a horse corral, old and worn down, with trees growing all around an old stable. You see this fence here, Chris? If you ever walk that fence, and it's very hard to do, and go over downhill, well there's another point down there, between two more arroyos – thirteen acres in all, and you only ever see about two and a half ... that property is probably worth two, three million dollars by now!'

I stared at the album as he flicked the pages. Howard with his first wife in the house they lived in before they separated . . . Howard's University laboratory with some of the equipment he built . . . Howard, by now shaven, with a tanned, healthy-looking, laughing girl standing beside him in the Caribbean . . .

'Isn't that Rose?' I asked.

'Rose Seeger, you remember her?'

'I was there when she moved in to your annexe. And the other girl moved out. Lowrie?'

'Yeah, Lowrie Fredericks. All that must have been happening when you were there. Right.'

Howard flicked over a few more pages, consigning Rose and Lowrie to the past (except that I had surnames to put to them now). A few more friends and Tellier relatives looked out at us; but mostly, page after page, they were photographs of Topside. He pointed out the old wagon-road that came down as far as the driveway, and the stile he used to climb over every morning with his bicycle over his shoulder that he'd push up the pasture to Campus Drive –

'Who was the Captain? You spoke about the old Captain who –'

'Captain Paginhart. And he was a real Captain! In the US Navy, before World War Two. A full Captain with full privileges, a licensed engineer and cartographer. Head of mapmaking for the US Navy for the whole of the Pacific between the wars.'

'So he actually built that place?'

Howard had obviously thought a lot about Captain Paginhart, a man after his own heart. He'd taken early retirement to come back to the West Coast, and the question he asked himself was – Where's the best place? Where do I want to be? He'd travelled the whole world, and when he came to Monterey Bay he stopped and looked around and tested the weather coming in, and started hunting for prime *filet mignon*, the best site on the Bay. He looked at Monterey and Carmel, and then he came up the coast to Santa Cruz.

What Captain Paginhart found, as Howard told me, was a piece of land he could afford to buy for back taxes, because there was nothing there. An eroded arroyo next to a cliff, and a bunch of scrub oak: it couldn't be farmed. An engineer by training, the Captain set to work and cleared the land. He built the driveway, laid the drains and had the house built so as to take best advantage of the view. He sent his children to high school in Santa Cruz, and ran for Mayor. Best of all, he laid out the garden.

'He was President of the Santa Cruz Garden Club for twenty years. The Club used to come there, to Topside. Because the garden was fabulous. I mean, it went all the way out to the point, and there were little walkways down. You can see what kind of garden he had because it still has exotic plants in it, and wire pipes on top of the old fences which came down and watered it all —'

'Used to,' I interrupted, thinking of what was there now.

'And you know, after I left Spring Street and went to New York — I was living by myself in the cold of a New York winter — I thought to myself — *What have I done?* I'd left this paradise, literally this paradise on earth where I was master — why? And what I kept telling myself was, the lesson that I've learned has really been the lesson of people . . .'

'How do you mean?'

Howard paused and called out to his wife, 'Tessa, can you bring that bottle of wine?' He refilled both our glasses and sat down again. 'Because, when I started that place, I thought it was going to be a kind of utopia, you know?'

Howard had looked out from his marvellous new home over the rose-garden and the sea and had been seized with the optimism which generations of Americans had had before him, that within the perfect natural landscape he could create a perfect human society. He thought of three or four people he'd got to know since coming to live in Santa Cruz, good friends who would share his vision of a utopian commune, and he had them all come over to the house one night. Howard's voice took on a hurt tone.

'Well, right away the problem was – Who's in charge? And there was tremendous friction because I had just assumed that I was. And of course they voted me out right away, first thing, within ten minutes. And I just said No . . . you know, just No.'

And so they fell to squabbling – about how duties would be shared between them, and who would pay what rent for different-sized rooms (it was six hundred dollars a month between six people: not an extortionate sum). One of Howard's friends backed out when he realized that he couldn't live in the same place as one of the others. A couple of others fell by the wayside because they didn't understand the basic rules of give-and-take which apply in a house-share. Within a matter of minutes Howard's friends were friends no longer.

I hadn't heard this story before. Perhaps by the time I knew him, Howard had come to realize that the two concepts were incompatible. Utopias you manufacture; paradises you stumble upon. Howard had tried to make a utopia out of Topside, somewhat along the lines of Rawls' first Theory of Justice, that everybody should have as much freedom as is compatible with an equal freedom for other people. But he quickly discovered that in practice human beings don't operate that way.

'So, I don't know,' Howard sighed, half-humorously. 'From right away in this perfect place I'd found, even before it was full, people started changing, there was turnover. At minus five countdown there was turnover! So eventually I realized that this couldn't be a commune. That was the lesson I learned – nowhere's perfect. Among other things I realized that if there was ever going to be any order, *I* would have to be the one to decide who was going to be there. I would pick the people and then I would filter, do a first cut. And then maybe I'd choose a couple more people, two, three, and after that the House would decide.'

Even that wasn't perfect. There were problems about people going away for weeks or months and having their friends and lovers to stay. Collecting rents from casual sublets became unmanageable, and that led to another condition – *Nobody else stays here* except for an occasional night or two. And of course that happened a lot, two or three nights a week, and the newcomer would be eating there, taking showers, hanging his laundry on the line . . . and that was why Howard eventually became weary of his would-be utopia, because it always threw up problems to which, as he said to me,

'There was no solution without you being so tough that the whole purpose of the enterprise was lost.'

Tessa was wheeling Gregory to the table for lunch. I said, 'Let me take you back to that summer. The people I remember – maybe you will too. There was someone called Rick who was studying Chinese History . . .'

'Rick Wanamaker. Rick was – is – a very bright guy.

Very Jewish. Rick and I had a sort of uneasy alliance, you know. He was . . . he really had all the bourgeois instincts of the master of the house, and he had made his own way in the world and had very great definiteness of purpose, which wasn't always a purpose I could agree with.'

Howard fell silent. I hadn't remembered any antagonism between the two of them; though, now that I thought about it, Howard and Rick could hardly have been more different.

'I always thought of Rick as . . . he always sort of threw a damp rag on things,' Howard continued. 'But on the other hand, when there were problems in the house, the kind of flare-up that happened from time to time, Rick was always a voice of reason, absolutely and independently. There were some tough jobs we had to do, and he pitched right in. I have a picture of him somewhere out in the garden – he helped create the best garden we ever had there. He put on his little Mao hat and his China shorts and he went out and dug in the garden like . . . the *masses*, you know.'

'Anyway, that was Rick. Then there was Andrea.' I wanted to move Howard on, greedy to fill the giant gaps in my memory. But my ex-landlord, who had spoken candidly enough about Rick Wanamaker, seemed strangely reluctant to discuss Andrea – Andrea *Rush* – except in terms of the house and how she had defined her part of it. He talked about her spectacular glass sun-room with its cathedral-like ceiling coming down ('Andrea was the only person who really grew into that suite of rooms'); he described the rainbow decal on the car she drove; he allowed that she was a woman of tremendous energy ('What she did to those rooms!'). But he had nothing personal to say about the woman who must surely have been the most memorable of all his tenants in Topside. Or were there other feelings there which he wasn't prepared to talk about?

'When Andrea left, Rick moved upstairs into the master bedroom,' Howard said. 'But it was never classy the way Andrea's room was.'

Tessa had been laying the table. She called us over to eat. She'd cooked up some nut cutlets (*nut cutlets? Howard?*) and produced a good plain simple salad, all the while coping with Gregory who was perched in his high chair at the top of the table, contentedly chewing away. A quiet-mannered woman, she was clearly devoted to her husband, proud of his intellect and his energy, protective of his boyish enthusiasms. Constantly she sought him out with her eyes as we sat at table, smiling tolerantly when he broke into what she was saying.

We talked about UCSC. Howard had come from a state college where science had been taught in compartments of maths, physics and chemistry, like high school. At UCSC for the first time in his life he was able to put everything together – a physical chemist who was becoming a physicist, listening to his fellow graduate students talking about physics and salting it away to integrate into his own studies. This was the man who had gone on to work in quantum optics, developing a clock which was many times more accurate than the atomic clock. Perhaps I could have predicted this from the intellectual passion which Howard brought to everything he discussed in Spring Street: but Howard had managed to apply his intellect in a way no non-scientist could.

I remembered the conversations people used to have back in the sixties about the alternative paths of Apollo and Dionysus, reason and passion. The University of Chicago, where C. had started his Paradise study, had been Apollonian and controlled to a fault. UCSC was Dionysian like there was no tomorrow. It gave the impression that life wasn't about order and clarity, but about letting your mind hang loose and just enjoying what went on.

'Yes, and if you look at the people who went up there, too.' That was a dig from Tessa, who had gone to Berkeley. The better part of UCSC's reputation, we agreed, was for letting people put their heads together and keep the ideas flowing.

'Or drift off into oblivion,' said Howard.

He'd gone off to New York, after Santa Cruz, and found himself a house on Long Island. But Katie, then in her mid-teens, was running wild and taking drugs, and both sets of her grandparents were back in the Bay Area of San Francisco. Howard realized that the only way to get a grip on his life was to bring Katie back so that she could be looked after better, while he found himself a post at Berkeley.

This was where things finally came together for him. He met Tessa, the step-daughter of his Professor at Berkeley, and married her. He took on a research project for the US government, and made the breakthrough which led to the creation of an immensely fine ceramic film for the blades of jet engines. This ceramic film retained thirty per cent more heat than any jet engine had been able to hold before – with a saving in fuel costs which transformed the economies of aircraft manufacturers.

It was one of the most exciting periods in Howard's life. It took him out of the poorly paid academic world into industry, first to a plant north of Richmond, then to his present company in Palo Alto. It was a success story. Tessa handed round the raisin-and-nut biscuits. We took our coffee and went back to the living-room.

'It's strange, you know, you coming here,' said Howard suddenly. 'I've been thinking a lot about that house, the effect it had on people.'

'On me? Did you think?'

'Oh sure. You were pretty quiet when you arrived. But, I seem to recall – it didn't take you long to fit in.'

'And it had an effect on you.'

'Yes. Oh sure. You know, the Captain and Nannie. That was his wife.'

'Did you meet them? Was that how you got to be there?'

Howard hesitated. 'Well, it's a funny story,' he said.

The Paginharts lived at Topside until they were in their early eighties. Then, in 1974, the Captain, trying to move some big rocks away from a culvert under the driveway, had an internal haemorrhage and was confined to his bed. His wife Nannie, an old-fashioned little Southern gentle-woman, was going blind, but she could still get about.

For a time she looked after the Captain. In due course, when it became too much for her, the three children – now all grown up and moved away from the West Coast – brought in a nurse to take care of the old man. Nannie sent her packing; she sent them all packing; she wasn't prepared to tolerate another woman in the house. So the Paginhart children brought in a Chinese boy, a graduate student from the University. He lived in the cottage and cut the grass and helped Nannie with the Captain, and if they needed to buy groceries or call a taxi or an ambulance he'd do that.

Then Nannie fell down and broke her hip. The Paginhart children descended swiftly and took the two of them off to an old folks' home.

'So now the Chinese guy's by himself in that cottage,' went on Howard, warming to his story. 'And he's *lonely*. He starts going nuts. It's cold and it's rainy. Winter. There's an empty house full of all their possessions he's supposed to take care of and guard – and I can just see this guy going around staring at the Captain's maps of the China Seas . . . Meanwhile I'm in this cellar in a house full of people down on High Street, and I'm dying. I'm sick as a dog with pneumonia, lying on a mattress, with the rain coming in through the basement window. I need a free place to live.'

An acquaintance in Howard's chemistry lab knew the Chinese man and how lonely he was. He called Howard up and told him he might have a place for him to live. Howard made arrangements to go and meet the Chinese student at Topside. It was springtime, and the sun was out, and the house looked beautiful. But the Chinese guy wasn't there. He had gone down to look at Howard's room in the basement of the house on High Street. By that time it was dry and warm; the house was full of friendly people, and he was invited to stay to dinner. He loved the dinner; he loved the deal – five bucks rent, and eat with twenty people every night; you cook once a week, otherwise your time's your own. Howard went up to live at Topside without ever meeting anybody who lived in it. It wasn't surprising that he felt as if he belonged there and it belonged to him.

One Sunday, the Paginharts came back, Nannie in a wheelchair. They told him about the garden and about the life they'd led . . . Howard lowered his voice and looked at me gravely.

'So now I know all the *history*, and I'm the only one who does.'

He never saw them again. Howard planted and tended

47

the rose-bushes, following their instructions. Then the Captain died, and it was two weeks before Nannie, who was drifting in and out of time present, had a good day and said to the Paginhart children, 'Let's go see the Captain.'

'The Captain's gone,' they told her.

'Captain's gone? I guess I'll go be with the Captain.' And within twenty-four hours she was dead.

I looked at Howard as he finished the story. The tears were streaming down his face. It began to dawn on me just how much the Captain and Nannie had meant to this toughly independent man. They had bestowed on Howard gifts which nothing in his experience had prepared him for. Gifts of rootedness and pride in ownership. Of belonging to somewhere that had a history. From his orphaned state in a damp basement, coughing his lungs up, they had raised him to the status of a favourite child and treated him to an inheritance that was all his own. In return and unknown to those two good old people, Howard had adopted them.

The house was quiet. Gregory was sleeping off his lunch. Howard coughed and made a grab for the photo-album.

'This is a group of us in my last summer in Spring Street, having a barbecue. And this is New York. Katie and I, and the house we lived in out on Long Island.'

I gazed at Katie, by then a teenager – big dark eyes and sloe-black hair framing the pale oval of her face.

'She's beautiful,' I said.

'Yes. You should go see Katie. I have her address somewhere. She could tell you things about then. There's a lot she hasn't forgotten.' Howard paused and cleared his throat. 'But you can see, I got really worked up by that story, because it's . . . the *magic* that was inside that place.'

He shook his head, lost in reverie.

'Captain,' he said softly. 'Captain and Nannie.'

*   *   *

We talked a bit more before I left, carefully disentangling ourselves from the past as if it were a bramble bush and we'd been caught blackberrying. Howard didn't know Phil, the present landlord of Topside. But before I left, rather unexpectedly he produced a telephone number for Lowrie Fredericks, his old girlfriend, in Aptos next door to Santa Cruz. Tessa gave me a kiss and a bag of her home-made cookies. Howard and I shook hands, solemnly. As I drove away, with Elysian Fields Drive below me, I saw him start digging in the ploughed earth at the back, on the steep slope which led up to the main road. He was getting ready to put a fence up and plant some vines along. Then he'd put some French windows in, and maybe a patio if there was room. The past was another country; he was pushing on, he had work to do.

I thought about him: his new house, his new family, his new identity as a company man. His field was the miniaturization of energy; he was working on a twenty-first-century car, built out of a near-zero-weight hollow tubing strengthened by inflated bladders, which would do the equivalent of one thousand miles to the gallon. He personified his own research: a dynamo of ideas and restless determination, an intellectual Daniel Boone pitting his wits against the physical universe with as much confidence as the early settlers had pitted their strength against the Rocky Mountains, looking for water and discovering gold.

My own confidence was a tad shaken. Memory had rubbed away the warmth and quickness of the man, the little quirks and mannerisms, and presented him as a *type* – the womanizing landlord, the motorbike-riding scientist who dabbled with drugs. Instead he'd turned out to be serious and disconcertingly sensitive to the spirit of the place. I'd underestimated him. I was going to have to be more careful.

But the *magic* . . . I wasn't satisfied that I'd got to the source of that. Andrea, she was the next one I needed to talk to. 'The real thing about Andrea *Rush*, she was the only person who really grew into the suite of rooms at the end,' so Howard had said. And he'd given me a lead. He thought he'd heard that Andrea was at the University of California at Berkeley, as a lecturer or associate professor.

In other words, less than ten miles away.

I'd rung from Howard's. Berkeley gave me an office number for Andrea; I left a message on her tape. This was proving simpler than I'd expected. Quest is an evocative word. It implies endurance and tenacity, the weary pursuit of a possibly unattainable goal, and the courage to overcome constant setbacks and disappointments on the way. It's true that Childe Harold wasn't on the telephone; Sir Gawain the Green Knight didn't have an automobile and a charge-card. But this was a piece of cake.

It was late afternoon. I parked on campus and looked Andrea up in the Register. Sure enough – *Andrea Rush, Ph.D. Associate Professor, Department of Social Ecology. Giannini Hall.* I walked down through the lawns and groves until I arrived at Giannini, and went up to the third floor.

Andrea's door was locked. Pinned up on a board was a schedule of her office tuition times. Strange – she should have been finishing up her teaching right now. I knocked. No answer. I saw the fanlight above the door was dark and turned away. The corridor was suddenly empty. I located the Department office a few doors down and tried the handle. It too was locked; nobody answered my banging, although I could see a light above the door.

Obviously Andrea hadn't got the message I left. It was Thursday; she probably took Thursday off, that was okay. I needed to stay here in Berkeley to talk to Katie Tellier. I'd get in touch with Andrea tomorrow, and give myself more time with her.

I walked back across the grass. The evening air was lemony. Serious-minded children with time on their side floated down the paths. They carried books with both their hands, like cherished objects from a lost culture. In front of me a kid of about eighteen, hair in a pony-tail, stopped the girl he was walking with. He lifted the strap of his book-bag over her head, binding them together in a scholarly embrace, and kissed the tip of her tongue.

I was seven thousand miles from home.

*   *   *

It had all begun with a kiss. C. was in his first job, as a junior editor in the London publishing house of Faber and Faber. This was where T. S. Eliot had spent nearly all his professional life, attending Faber board meetings in a clerical-grey suit and overseeing its incomparable poetry list. By the time C. arrived Eliot was four years dead, but on his first day he was proudly shown the office Eliot used, the chair he sat in, the mahogany hat-stand on which he hung his coat and muffler. Hallowing his memory, Fabers organized an annual series of T. S. Eliot Lectures which took place in Canterbury at the University of Kent.

His first year, C. had travelled down with his fellow-editors in the train and the special bus laid on for the company outing. This year he had a car, and somebody he wanted to impress. Her name was Nilzete. She was the daughter of a Brazilian diplomat who had been assigned to the Court of St James a short while before. C. met her on a picnic, and fell in love.

On a cold March day, wearing his best suit (by then one size too small, the salary of a junior commissioning editor being only slightly more than one might expect to make playing the mouth-organ outside Russell Square underground station), C. drove down to Canterbury. Nilzete sat beside him, dressed in shocking-pink, with a skirt which rode up her thighs. Inexpressible was his joy and pride. Nilzete had the kind of beauty which exploded in your face: large dark eyes, a wide mouth, adorable features set in a perfect oval face, with lustrous hair and skin the colour of Greek honey. As sensuous as a sleepy kitten, she was the only person C. had ever known who would create a silence around her simply by entering a room.

Other women have been as heart-stoppingly beautiful. The difference was that Nilzete carried off her beauty with such unselfconsciousness that it seemed to confound the natural order of things. Male friends of his whom C. introduced her to went into deep shock, surmising that, Pygmalion-like, C. had breathed life into their most secret fantasy of womanhood. Only when Nilzete began to talk to them, her broken English giving her sentences an amused and cryptic resonance, did they unfreeze into common envy and normal conversation resumed.

Before stepping across the wintry yard to join the lecturegoers in the auditorium, the directors of Faber and

Faber were taking sherry with their underlings in the rooms of the Master of Eliot College. Middle-aged men in sober apparel, their pinstripes cross-hatched by the curve of gold watch-chains across billowy waistcoats . . . a few women in long thin frocks. Escorted by Faber's most junior editor, Nilzete entered the room like something from outer space. Sherry glasses froze in the air.

C. looked around. His heart sank. He'd thought that he would be taking Nilzete to meet the distinguished people he worked with, but he'd got it the wrong way round. Nilzete was the distinguished one. In every graceful movement, every gesture and expression, she radiated the distinction of her youth, her beauty, her vitality, her freedom. How could C. have supposed that he would be doing *her* any favours, taking her, in this company, to sit through George Steiner lecturing at length on his latest redefinition of European culture?

Wretchedly did C. introduce Nilzete around the room to colleagues who were contorting with the effort of adjusting their image of him to accommodate the shocking-pink apparition by his side. Wretchedly did he escort her to their seats halfway down the auditorium to listen to Professor Steiner describe the effects of the Holocaust on Western cultural values. Sunk in despair C. listened to him declare that Hell was more interesting than Heaven, because representations of Paradise could only illustrate a suicidal contentment. So what? But at that moment Nilzete, beautiful forgiving Nilzete, leant over in full view of the billowy waistcoats and nibbled and licked his ear.

C. shot half out of his seat. Despair fled; he was electrified with joy. His love for Nilzete, his gratitude, was unbounded. Mentally lighting a candle to the Muses, there and then he vowed that he would prove Paradise was anything but boring; and that it was as much about bodily joy as about spiritual bliss. Every torment of Hell, which had stirred the ghoulish imaginings of artists and writers across the centuries, he would match with a sensory pleasure which evoked the delights of Paradise.

But whose Paradise? Almost every religious faith has its myth of an elysium to which those who are brave and good pass on to receive their everlasting reward. For Islam it is jewelled gardens of Eden full of food and drink and girls with swelling breasts. For Buddhists it is a state of oneness and stillness way up above the whirligig of birth and dying. Every thinking being has a dreamtime, a transcendental alternative to life on earth. For all C. knew, his old and smelly beagle at home in Kent dreamt of a paradise of gently rotting bones. As he filed out of the lecture-hall with Nilzete, his arm proprietorially round her waist as though he had done something to deserve her ostentatious intimacy, it occurred to him that he had one particular obligation to fulfil. All the spiritual and intellectual pleasures of his life – music, art, philosophy – had derived from a Christian culture. So had the women in his life, however disapproving the Church would have been.

C. always said that that's how he lighted upon Paradise. I don't believe it myself. I think it was darker and more complicated than that. Howsoever, the Christian versions of Paradise became a theme and a preoccupation for him which lasted for seven years, across two continents, associated forever with a dream of fair women. Nilzete slipped through his fingers, as she was fated to do. She had to go home to Bahia – or so she told him, although when C. next heard of her, some years later, she was happily married to an American millionaire whose company made suits a great deal smarter than his. C. left publishing for a job in journalism. When Fabers moved from its Georgian town-house in Russell Square to a modern office-block, he bought T.S. Eliot's chair off the firm for £5, and had it re-upholstered.

        *   *   *

'Now then, you say you'd use one of these Fellowships to go out and research into ideas of Paradise. Isn't this the kind of work you could do as well or better here in England?'

'Er, I don't think so. After all, America was founded as a second Eden. There's a consciousness that Paradise is more than a metaphor for many Americans; it's a standard set for them by the Founding Fathers . . .'

It was the kind of answer which is tailored to interview-boards. But the odd thing was, C. meant it. Not that coming out to America could have made any difference to his academic research. It didn't. But for himself, he needed to escape into a realm of possibilities. God gave man a second chance in America: that's what the early colonists believed. Like them, and generations who followed them, C. wanted to renew his faith in the possibility of Faith.

Nobody could call the Britain of the early and mid-1970s a golden age. Even before the oil ran out it was becoming a mean, impoverished, resentful society, living under governments which taxed individual enterprise in the cause of social engineering and scoffed at anything which couldn't be proved on a slide-rule. While union leaders were having tea and sandwiches with the Prime Minister at 10 Downing Street, half their work-forces were out on strike.

Christopher Hudson

Educationalists were telling teachers and pupils that it was wrong to compete, elitist to excel, authoritarian to teach facts because that gave some kids an advantage over others: instead classes should be allowed to develop their creative instincts in an unstructured way. The key word was play, although the young victims of this iniquitous system had been deprived of the framework of knowledge on which to build and create.

What a weary cynicism was in the air! We who had been so fiercely committed to individual freedoms in the 1960s, we who had marched on Grosvenor Square to protest the war in Vietnam, we who had bought the first underground magazines, smoked the first joints, worn the first off-the-peg velvet jackets, listened to the first Beatles records, spoken out for free love and hollered our joyous disbelief at the Old Bailey trial of Penguin for publishing *Lady Chatterley's Lover* – we found our battles won so easily that the freedoms hardly seemed to have been worth fighting for. In the sea-wall of bourgeois convention that had surrounded our childhoods, where we had made the breach and seen the tempestuous waters rushing in, now all was flat, calm, placid acceptability.

C. hadn't forgotten his promise to the Muses. What was starting to worry him was the thought that George Steiner might have been right. It was easy enough to sneer at John Martin's visionary canvases on exhibition at the Tate Gallery – his *Fields of Heaven* with its nymphs prancing in an English meadow and the domes of a celestial city poking unconvincingly through the clouds in the background – but actually what were the alternatives?

C. scribbled sombrely in his notebook:

'The pictures of Hell have always been more detailed.

Presumably we can re-create what makes us endlessly suffer more easily than what makes us endlessly happy because happiness needs continual reminders of its opposite, while pain needs no comparisons to get its message across. Delight is a thing of excess, of extremes. How can it be captured in words or pictures, when to expose it to permanence is to expose it to reflection, scepticism, analysis, the vocabulary of human limitation?'

And in his own life C. was struggling to hold on to the possibility of delight. On the surface of things (and he was spending his time on the surface of things) he had it all. C. had been the youngest commissioning publisher in London: now he was the youngest literary editor, and for a weekly journal internationally famous for its political astringency and acerbic wit. To its London parties came Cabinet Ministers, celebrated novelists, chairmen of arts organizations, top businessmen, the leading right-of-centre press and TV commentators of the day. This particular party, in the journal's magnificent Regency boardroom, C. was hosting jointly with the Editor-in-Chief.

C. moved graciously among his invited guests, dispensing courtesies. It was gratifying to see how the Establishment in Britain comported itself on these social occasions. Politicians who in public were seen to disagree violently over issues such as strike-breaking and coloured immigration were chuckling together, evidently the best of friends. Journalists who attacked them consistently in print went up and shook their hands with every sign of affection. Among these people – most of them older than C. was – arguments were avoided by the customary English ploy of gossiping about important matters and taking seriously only the trivial ones.

Four years down from university C. was just learning to

do the same. Contented, he gazed around the room. Hunched in a corner by the door, his back to the wall, stood one of his oldest friends, a contemporary who in the 1980s was to achieve an international reputation as a playwright and film-maker. Sourly and silently he was surveying the party. Beside him, the guest he'd brought along looked more miserable even than the Hamlet he'd recently played at Stratford-upon-Avon to universal acclaim.

C. strolled over to them to see if they wanted anything. His old friend from Cambridge studied him scornfully.

'Look around you,' he said.

C. looked around.

'Is this what it's all about?' he went on. 'Can't you see anything *wrong*?'

C. told him that he was addicted to the politics of envy, and got him another drink. What really vexed him was that he understood immediately what his friend was getting at. *He* knew who he was, and had kept faith with that, however grimly. In the company of cosmopolitan right-wingers C. was beginning not to know who he was any longer.

In the week that closed his first year as literary editor he penned a gloomy self-analysis in the notebook he was keeping. 'It seems to get harder all the time to achieve any of the real joy in life that came naturally even a year ago – in France, for instance, when it hardly seemed to matter whether I had a job, a house or a girlfriend to go back to or not. It may be just the process of getting older and having responsibilities which can't, at last, be neglected or cast off. But I continue to have done nothing, except through the medium of other people, and to be judged simply for what I am – and yet this identity, week by week, gets pared away

in the repetitions of acceptable social behaviour. I am getting
as smooth and round as a pebble.'

C. took a break in the Lake District. Alone on the
shoreline of Ullswater he skidded pebbles – *split, split, split*
– across the glittering surface until they sank and disappeared. Most of the private stuff he was writing had to do
with death. He had just finished a short television play,
based on Bartók's ballet *The Miraculous Mandarin*, about
a couple of nomads in a ghetto of decayed and burning
tenements, robbing and pimping to get together the fare to
the promised land beyond the Control Zone. A mix of
science fiction and fairy-tale, it featured a beautiful but
simple-minded hooker and a customer who loves her and
disguises himself as a guru to rescue her from the pimps.
Everybody gets murdered except the girl, by now deranged,
who's to be seen at the end, in a Polanski-style wide-angle,
wheeling her dead lover across mud-flats towards the never-
never land.

Looking back at him I simply don't recognize this solitary,
pessimistic young Werther, one minute holding his head in
his hands in despair at the illogicality of the universe, the
next minute putting on a jacket and tie and going in to the
office to write film reviews and edit books pages. One thing
about him for sure: he was undergoing some sort of spiritual
crisis.

People in their twenties in every generation go through
similar pangs of rootlessness and despair. It remains the
case, I think, that my late 1960s generation, brought up
with love and fresh orange juice into the first genuinely
secular society, was unusually impressionable. The world
was too much with us – its glitzy materialism, its instant
news on wrap-around TV, its pervasive joke of nuclear

oblivion – and since we were the first to encounter these things, we had no defences built. Nor, except for a tiny Christian minority, was there still the compensation of belief in a better world to come. If God was alive, he was no longer to be trusted. Systems of belief had produced the mad, mad world we lived in: communism, fascism, rival religions. The only sensible response was to reject all systems, and fall back on the lonely pursuit of self-knowledge. Self-knowledge was the utmost we could hope to achieve as a touchstone of the truth of things.

The logic of this theory was impeccable. I still find it appealing. Unfortunately it didn't get most of us very far in practice, whatever distances we travelled in quest of it, out to Katmandu or inwards through layers of personality peeled back like an orange by therapy or LSD.

Self-knowledge didn't help to make intellectual sense of a world which refused to make sense on any level. People C. knew quite well were killing themselves for apparently casual reasons. One of his flat-mates in Covent Garden, haunted by delusions of persecution, bought a whole lot of slippers and placed them in single footprints towards the door of his room. Another provided a twenty-first birthday present of a shot of methadone to a punk heroin-addict who used to come round to their rooms and lay her life-story on them as she combed out her brittle hair with her guitar plectrum. All the while, in a parallel universe, government ministers were coming to lunch at the Gower Street offices of the magazine to discuss electricity strikes, incomes policies, the European Economic Community and Britain's shrinking role in world affairs.

A book came C.'s way for review, about Paradise. It turned out to be a novel by Michael Frayn called *Sweet*

Dreams, about a middle-class achiever called Howard. Driving home from a drinks party Howard is killed in a crash on Highgate Hill and finds himself transported to a Heaven populated by the kind of person C. recognized only too well: a complacent liberal whose progress from radicalism to conservatism was disguised by self-satisfaction at the moral and intellectual example he set to others.

Howard, as far as I can remember the story, is suddenly struck by the moral ambiguity of his way of life in Heaven, and moves out to lead the simple life in the depths of the countryside. By this time C. had done the same. He'd left his literary editorship on the magazine and abandoned London to go and live in the Oxfordshire village of Woodstock, in a half-timbered set of rooms overlooking the graveyard. He didn't want to submit to the Protestant ethic of marriage and mortgage and the nine-to-five working day, if this was the company he would have to keep.

The snapshot I have of him shows a curiously uncontoured face, thick-lipped, staring-eyed, with an unhealthy pallor. It's the eyes I don't like. There's no amusement in them. C. had been shooting in the dark too long. Opening the *Sunday Times* he read a Gallup Poll which said that for the third year running, Edward Heath had alternated with Harold Wilson for the title of the most popular man in Britain, with Prince Philip as the runner-up. That same day he wrote away to the Harkness Foundation for his forms to apply for a fellowship to the United States.

      *   *   *

A grey day in the Mission district of San Francisco. The streets were as grey as the battleships they're named after –

York, Alabama. I was on my way to see Katie, Howard Tellier's daughter. She'd been eleven years old in 1976 – a child in paradise, in the paradise of childhood. I tried to imagine what it must have been like for her. After all, it is one of the oldest and most pervasive themes in the literature of the Western world that paradise is associated with the unknowing of childhood. Wordsworth takes it up and turns it into some of his finest poetry. So does Blake. When they write about their childhood, their poetry is suffused with religious imagery, because they are returning their thoughts to the closest they have known to an earthly paradise. 'It is like a residue in us of a primitive state of mind,' writes M. Cazeneuve in his book *Happiness and Civilization.* 'Too greatly civilized, we lessen the strain by linking our own infancy with the infancy of humankind.'

Adam and Eve are often presented to us as childlike – being, after all, in a state of sexual innocence. I had just started re-reading some of the early Paradise material which C. had been working on. What I hadn't realized was that the precise degree of Adam's innocence was crucial to the battle fought by the early Christian Church against paganism.

The distinction between good and evil, between the forces of light and the forces of darkness, is at the heart of most pagan religion. The early Christians faced an uphill struggle to persuade people to believe in the existence of a God who was all-powerful enough to encompass good *and* evil. The concept of a Paradise of the faithful was necessary to attract believers, but it was a double-edged weapon. Too much emphasis on Paradise – as a pleasure-garden, as a Peaceable Kingdom, even as a celestial community of saints – and the Church would be back fighting off the old dualism between good and evil which God was supposed to overcome.

The biblical story of Eden and the Fall was a crucial text in the battle between paganism and Christianity. It is there in Genesis, plain for all to read, but where did it spring from? What did it mean? Like all myth, it must have come into currency in a pre-literate age, to provide imaginative answers to questions which couldn't be answered by experience. As the questions changed, down the centuries, so does the interpretation of the myth change in response.

This is true of the Genesis story, as C. discovered in Chicago. The text stays the same but everything else changes, even the physical nature of its leading characters. In the Middle Ages, Adam and Eve tend to appear as tiny, insect-like creatures in the margins of illuminated manuscripts, not becoming human and lifelike until the Renaissance, when people for the first time found the courage and self-esteem to look God in the face. At the genesis of Genesis they were pawns in a quite different game.

The so-called Jahwist story-teller who composed what we know as Chapters 2 and 3 of the Old Testament book of Genesis, relying on oral traditions handed down from generation to generation, had another purpose in mind for Adam and Eve than the one Christians are familiar with. Historians believe that he was gathering his material probably in the tenth century BC, not long after the first Hindu book of sacred knowledge, the *Rig-Veda*, and about a century before the *Iliad*. More significantly, the Jahwist was operating at roughly the same time as King Solomon's temple was being built on Mount Zion, and his purpose was similar – to assert the absolute God-given right of the Hebrew tribes to the land of Canaan.

To do this meant concocting a plausible explanation for the defeats and misfortunes of the Hebrews in the past. If the Hebrew God Jahweh had a purpose in bringing them to the Promised Land, he must have had a purpose in allowing them to suffer in the first place. The Israelites could not have been pointlessly condemned: they must have brought their sorrows upon themselves. The disobedience of Adam and Eve, and the crime of their son Cain, was a means to explain the purpose of Jahweh's covenants with Abraham and Moses. He had punished the Israelites; now he would console them and reward them with the land of Canaan.

It doesn't matter where the Jahwist author went for his prototypes. They were common enough in Babylonian myth. The story of the deceitful serpent stealing the plant of immortality from the unthinking king is told with unforgettable poetry on the eleventh tablet of the *Epic of Gilgamesh*, the most ancient of all heroic poems. The point is that the Old Testament Garden in Eden was different in kind as well as degree from all the Gardens of Eden that followed. Before the early Church connected it with Christ's sacrifice on the Cross, it was simply a mythical oasis protected from the drifting sands, 'well-watered everywhere' like the land God showed to Moses. In the ancient Babylonian tongue Eden means 'wilderness', and the Eden outside the Garden would have been familiar enough to the Jahwist author, or to the exiled audiences of Isaiah and Ezekiel. The ground was hard. It yielded little besides thistles and thornbushes. It was the desert in which the tribes of Israel had wandered for years before God rescued them.

The modern Garden of Eden, which so resembles the earthly paradise, was invented one thousand years later, to meet a different but equally pressing challenge. In the first centuries after Christ, the simple Hebrew nationalism of the Jahwist story-teller was not the issue: the Eden story had another role to play. The early Christian Church found itself locked in a power-struggle against rival cults, the mystery-religions of Greece and Rome. If Christianity had not managed to demonstrate how different and how novel it was, it would have been engulfed in the confusion and pessimism of pagan beliefs in the late Roman Empire.

The Church's most powerful weapon was the Scriptures, and this is where the Genesis narrative played such a crucial part. The pagan cults were essentially dualist. They shared a deep-rooted belief in the ancient separation between light and darkness, spirit and matter, goodness and evil in the universe. What Christianity had to offer was a single all-powerful God who created Man as indivisible body-and-soul, and linked his fate to the whole past and future history of mankind.

Saint Paul in his first letter to Corinth had written about Christ as a second Adam come to redeem the sins of the first. It established the doctrine that the story of the Fall of Man was linked in all its details to Man's redemption by Christ on the Cross. No longer was God's Covenant just with his chosen people, giving them the Holy Land. After Christ's death it became a new Covenant with all those who believed in him as the Son of God. In this new scenario the Garden of Eden became an earthly paradise, lost at the beginning of history in order that it might be won back at the end by the elect of God.

On the absolute plausibility of this series of connections rested the success or failure of Christianity in the late Roman Empire. This is why the Eden story was constantly being redefined and reinterpreted by successive Fathers of the Church, as shrewdly as any Communist ideologues re-phrasing the party line in the light of current political realities.

For instance, there was a real danger that too realistic a preview of the paradise to come might direct the thoughts of Christians away from contemplation of the goodness of God. Too seductive a vision of the future could be dynamite in the hands of some rabble-rouser promising instant salvation. Besides, it stretched the credulity of many Christian scholars to read into the Fall story a historical statement about the origins of man. 'Who is so silly,' wrote the third-century Alexandrian theologian Origen, in some impatience, 'as to believe that God, after the manner of a farmer, "planted a paradise eastward in Eden", and set in it a visible and palpable "tree of life", of such a sort that anyone who tested the fruit with his bodily teeth would gain life; and again that one could partake "of good and evil" by masticating the fruit taken from the tree of that name?'

Origen and the even more influential St Ambrose leant heavily on the allegorical, Platonic approach of another Alexandrian, Philo, a near-contemporary of Christ. Philo had interpreted the Jahwist account as an allegory on Man, in which Adam represented understanding, Eve sensation and the Serpent pleasure. St Ambrose went further – 'Paradise is the soul in which are planted the Virtues, and where the tree of life, that is Wisdom, is also to be found.' Add to this the argument of St Paul to the Ephesians that the Christian Church was itself a prototype of paradise on earth (which enabled the Church Fathers to declare that baptism represented the entry into Paradise) and it was no wonder that ordinary Christians were confused over what kind of beatitude they might expect as the reward for a virtuous life on earth.

C. had started out in Chicago looking for the golden thread which would lead him through the maze of Paradise imagery to the heart of the matter. But he found himself spending more and more time with these remarkable men, saints of the early Church, for whom a precise definition of Paradise, and the place of Adam and Eve therein, was not a pleasant academic excursion but a question of life-or-death significance. Once they had managed to overcome the pagan overtones of the story (it was such a powerful dramatization of good versus evil that it awakened the old dualist super-stitions) they had to grapple with the dialectical nightmare of Original Sin and the limitations which the Fall appears to place on Man's free will.

The idea that Man is predestined to sin as a consequence of Adam's Fall had been ascribed (inaccurately) to St Paul and was therefore the next best thing to Holy Writ. But it was hard to swallow: at any rate for those scholars who preferred the application of logic over blind faith in 'revelation'.

The early Christian debate on the nature of Original Sin was deeply divided over the nature of free will. On one side were such commentators as Tertullian and Clement of Alexandria. They held that there was nothing evil about the Tree of Knowledge or its fruit, and the problem lay with Adam and Eve, who were too infantile to use the knowledge wisely. On the other were scholars like Basil the Great, Gregory of Nyssa and Ambrose himself. They claimed that God would never have attributed wrongdoing and guilt to a little child, and that on the contrary Adam was a kind of demi-god, who sinned by falling through pride from a state of original perfection.

It was St Augustine, early in the fifth century AD, who hit upon an acceptable compromise. He saw the dangers in both versions. If Adam had been infantile he could not be held fully responsible for the Fall. That would be to diminish the magnitude of his sin – which would give credence to the heretical followers of Pelagius, who preached that Man's fate was not predestined and could be redeemed by good works in this life. On the other hand, to give Adam and Eve demi-god status would mean giving equal status to Satan, or Lucifer, or whatever it was that had managed to trick our first parents in the disguise of a snake. It would hark back to the ancient dualism of goodness and evil as co-efficient forces in the universe.

The compromise worked out by St Augustine, in his writings and sermons, was so shrewdly defensive that it held firm for the next fourteen centuries. It enabled the Church to survive the collapse of the Roman Empire. St Thomas Aquinas accepted it. So did Milton in *Paradise Lost*. Adam and Eve, according to Augustine, were superhuman in their potential and childlike in their inexperience. They sinned through wilful disobedience; their punishment was aware-ness of what they had lost by sinning. Christians who lived their lives as if to expiate that original sin might be saved at the Last Judgement. All the others (which meant ninety-nine per cent of human kind) were predestined to eternal damnation.

In the Mission district the sun has come through the clouds, and it's not dowdy any more but shabby-picturesque, like students' quarters the world over. If innocence is bliss, then Katie had been doubly served by happiness. She could have had little idea of the extent to which Lucifer had carried temptation into Spring Street: the sexual unions and disunions . . . the drugs. She skipped through the summer days unembarrassed by guilt or shame, as I seemed to remember, conscious of nothing irksome on the horizon except the nuisance of homework.

I ring the door-bell of the tall grey-and-white house and squeeze past bicycles in the hall-way and up the cluttered stairs to the upper landing. The door opens on cats and screen-prints and drying clothes and a splash of red gardenias in a dusty window-box. A large girl in a loose shirt wanders out of a bedroom and back in again. In the middle of the living-room a man in overalls kneels on pages of the *San Francisco Chronicle* scraping the paint off a motor-bike. And this unrecognizable, beautiful girl is welcoming me in.

She had been eleven years old in Spring Street. Now she's twenty-four, Miss Katie Tellier, and I don't know what to say to her. Small-boned, ultra-slim, fashionably pale-cheeked, she's more waif-like than her picture in Howard's photograph album. Except, I notice, she handles herself with a carefulness that's older than her years. Anaemia, Howard had said. But her blood-cell count was normal, she'd told him so.

'You won't remember me,' I tell her fondly.

'Sure I do!' She sparkles palely at me. 'It's real nice you could come. Let's go in the kitchen, it's quieter, okay? Tell me about the book you're writing. Eric – this is my boyfriend Eric – he's just finished reading one of your books, *The Final Act*. He really enjoyed it, didn't you, Eric?'

'Yup,' says Eric, not looking up, scraping off the paint.

We sit at the kitchen table. I am introduced to Terry, the girl in the shirt whom she shares the apartment with, and asked what I'll have to drink.

'Coffee. Thanks.'

'Oh God. We don't have coffee. Tea? We've got rose-hip, blackberry or camomile.'

I settle for blackberry tea, with one sugar. Katie looks away with a twist of amusement at this eccentric British person. She opens cupboard doors and shuts them. She is reading Psychology at San Francisco University, so Howard told me, and teaching art therapy at the Children's Hospital in Oakland. In her spare time she designs patterns for printing on to silk, and is having some success marketing them. Howard has tried to persuade her to focus full-time on applied design, but she won't give up her course-work. It dates back to the 1970s, this determination. Katie became hooked on education in Spring Street because all the interesting people she met were in graduate school.

'Terry, do we have any sugar?'

'Sugar! We've never had sugar.'

'Christopher, I'm sorry. Will this do?'

Katie produces a sachet of powdered saccharine. I sprinkle it on the blackberry tea, and sip. It's good. I compliment her. Katie giggles.

'You know, it's really weird to see you!'

'You too. You were about eleven when I was in Spring Street.'

'I was?' She counts back on her fingers. 'My God! Eleven!' She cannot believe that she was ever eleven years old. 'I must have just started going to school.'

'To public school, yes. I remember thinking you were really enjoying getting into reading, writing and arithmetic. Math, I mean. After that Montessori school, what was its name?'

'Daybreak. They said they were Montessori . . . And I'd been to probably four before that!'

Little kids running free in Nature's wonderland . . . it all seemed ridiculously far away now. Katie does her best to remember. There would be a meeting in the morning, and the children and their instructors would sit round in a circle, as in some kind of group-therapy session. Sometimes there would be a special topic for the day. And once in a while, a long while, some kind of written assignment or math assignment would be given out, in case anybody felt like doing it. But the guiding principle was free expression.

I felt I knew what she was talking about. I could imagine that these were the sort of people who in the 1960s had been drop-outs, and who in the 1970s earned the money they needed to prolong their self-indulgence by passing on the message that play was the most important expression of human freedom. This must have seemed like pretty good wisdom to little children not old enough to know any better. I couldn't blame Katie for not having any desire to remove herself from this blissful existence and go to ordinary public school. But I didn't realize how painful it was for her. She laughs ruefully.

'You know, even being a hippie or an intellectual, Dad was still rather a severe character – and this was like the worst nightmare I could possibly imagine come true! And I remember that when I started at public school some of my teachers thought I was, like, mentally retarded! I still to this day – I don't know whether it's dyslexia or something – I still can't *spell*, you know. I have to use a Spell-check when I write anything; it's absolutely mandatory!'

She pours some more tea. When C. first moved in, she was still living in the cottage. The situation, as she delicately explains, wasn't set up for kids. Howard didn't expect suddenly to find his young daughter on his doorstep. There was nowhere for her to sleep, unless she shared the one bedroom. Nevertheless she got on really well with Howard at first, despite the business of her schooling. Lowrie was in the cottage, motherly Lowrie. But then Rose Seeger arrived. Lowrie moved out and Katie was sent over with her to the main house.

'I wasn't close with Rose at that time. There was a lot of antagonism there at first. So as it worked out it was actually kind of like a respite to have a lot of other people around. It served the function of . . . like an extended family, where the other people served to mediate.'

This is just how I seem to remember it: freedom within the security of an extended family; a little girl having the time of her life.

'It was a good thing, perhaps?' I suggest. 'It meant that instead of one person being very possessive of you, you could be treated as part of the whole group. That was my picture of you: as someone who was not *part* of anyone but just kind of independently there.'

But Katie isn't buying this. 'I think, in retrospect, being there as a child, and of that age, was not necessarily a good thing.' A rather wistful smile turns down the corner of her mouth. 'I think that if I'd had a stronger notion of family connections, perhaps of parenting, at least a notion of the kind of sanctuary that most children generally experience, I probably would have been a little bit more secure . . .'

'Oh.'

'By the same token there were a lot of things happening around me that were kind of destabilizing. Arguments that people would get in, especially Howard and Rose and Lowrie. I just thought that situation was . . . *pathetic*. You know? So in a way it was really nice to live with all these other people.'

A slap of slippers on the floorboards. Terry puts her head round the door to say that Marmalade is missing. Katie excuses herself, I sit over my blackberry tea, the smile fading on my face. This isn't the way it's supposed to be.

A couple of minutes later she's back. Marmalade has been sighted – Marmalade the cat.

'It amazes me,' says Katie, picking up on Spring Street, 'when I think back – how a lot of people in that house dealt with me on a level that made me feel an individual. I could be included in discussions, or just kind of hang out with people. And that seemed kind of surprising, considering that I wasn't really considered anyone's responsibility. You know – there was this kid!'

She looks at me with a sophisticated moue of self-deprecation and touches her hair. I notice her earrings, simple but graceful. Marmalade balances on the window-box, stares fiercely through the glass, and stalks away.

I wonder aloud whom she knew best, of all of us. Katie mentions the name of a girl called Kathy, who must have come to Spring Street after I'd left. Kathy she'd been a lot closer to than Howard. Another surrogate parent.

'But she moved out too. And yet it's funny, because I have really positive feelings about that house. It was like kind of mixed love and hate: because for example I couldn't invite friends over. It definitely was not a standard living situation.' Katie's mouth momentarily takes on the prim expression of a small girl trying terribly hard to match the conformism of her new friends who looked down their noses at the hippie life. 'Going to public school, everybody else had a standard household situation. I couldn't invite people over, other children in fifth and sixth grade, because there'd be people nude-sunbathing out in the yard!'

She grins. 'And yet by the same token Spring Street was this really wonderful refuge where there were a lot of people around who *didn't* hold standard notions of what was societally expected of children – or of anyone else for that matter – and I'm sure a lot of these attitudes have rubbed off on me. At the time, I hated it! I wanted to live in the suburbs, and have a nice feature of lawn and a clean driveway, you know? And a Mum and Dad who did socially acceptable things and didn't ride motorcycles!'

Laughter burbles in her voice like spring water. So much for the innocence of childhood, the paradise of unknowing. Katie didn't have time for innocence. She had to grow up fast. Spring Street hadn't represented the Garden of Eden to Katie: it represented expulsion into the wilderness.

'Instead you had all of us!' I say.

'Yes. I don't know if it was Spring Street, or the time I lived there, or perhaps even the perspective I had being a child, because I would be extremely aware when someone wasn't getting along or when there was bad energy or whatever. And it just kind of seemed ridiculous to me on some levels you know . . . the completely idiotic things that would happen to some of the adults living there.'

'What sort of things?'

'Well . . . you, for instance.'

'What about me?'

Katie gets it out. 'Your black eye!'

Oh God, I should have thought of that.

I say, 'Yes, that must have been a pretty funny sight.'

'No. I didn't think it was hilariously funny to see you looking like that. I remember how awful it was, and I remember that it was someone's lover that had given it to you!'

Katie giggles. I ask her about the others. I can't have been the only idiotic adult in Spring Street. Jan? Hélène? Rick?

'Oh, Rick, yes. Rick seemed perhaps a little bit withdrawn. I can remember him being in social situations and not really participating and feeling very uncomfortable and formal about things. I would be sitting in the living-room having dinner with groups of people and Rick would walk in with some woman – you know, they're obviously going to sleep together – and even if he was having arguments with people in the house, and probably hadn't said anything to them for days, he'd bring her over and introduce her to everybody!'

She giggles again, at the thought of Rick's East Coast good manners. At the same time she had a lot of respect for anyone who lived in Topside and didn't get along with her father. Rick was one. Andrea was another.

'That was one of the few sentiments I can remember having about Andrea, that she didn't get along with Dad very well and was outspoken, flamboyant . . . But this wild vision of Rick started going through my head as soon as you mentioned him. I used to incinerate the garbage, out beyond the edge of the garden, and there was Rick dressed up like someone out of the Chinese revolution. I mean he had a Mao badge on and he was out there with a hoe! Hoeing – it was so ridiculous!'

Katie can hardly get the words out, she's giggling so much. Chastened, I think back to all of us in Topside: our obsessions, our love affairs, our attempts at self-expression – and Katie had been grown-up enough not only to understand but to forgive! I think of my own childhood, when our elders were automatically our betters, and grown-up power and authority precluded any attempt to bridge the gulf of understanding.

'What about Andrea?' I ask, curious. 'You say she and Howard didn't get along very well?'

'That's right.' But Andrea, to my surprise, doesn't figure much in Katie's recollections of Spring Street, for reasons I don't come to appreciate until later. Andrea taught social anthropology at UCSC and held extramural classes in Women's Studies at Spring Street, which attracted to the house a motley collection of pioneering feminists, stridently man-hating lesbians and radical Marxists who ensured that feminist discussions were absorbed into a political argument. The Women's Group met in the living-room, and Katie resented the encroachment on her space, especially the meetings held by people who didn't even live at Topside.

And then the fieldwork – 'Andrea used to take a lot of trips, and I would go and hang out with her African artefacts and artwork while she was gone, and wander around looking at them and appreciating them – carvings and things like that.'

I ask to see some of her silk designs, the ones Howard had told me about.

Katie gets up and trips lightly into the living-room. In a moment she is back with a big colour photograph of herself robed in silks against a vivid background of silk rolls and drapes and hangings, the kind of designs I remember from Andrea's rooms. The colours are bold and rich, controlled by the elegance of her patterns, and Katie, modelling them, looks like a sculpted, alabaster Queen of Sheba.

I admire them. Katie smiles and shrugs her thin shoulders.

'I feel as if I'm kind of exploiting the Third World. All these African-style patterns on the backs of real rich people – I mean Miami matrons, you know?'

'Does it make any difference? I mean if your designs were mass-marketed, say on cheap cotton fabrics.'

'I don't know. I guess not. My creative input would be the same. And I enjoy doing the design work.'

And there's no question about it, these designs are good. Katie Tellier has real flair. Why should she bother to stay in graduate school when she could earn a living doing this full-time?

I put this to her. Katie gives me a wry look, as if to say – You need to ask? And, after everything she has told me, I see her point. There were no fixed points in her childhood, no framework on which to cling and grow. The Psychology major is part of the structure of her life that she's had to build from scratch. She's not going to take unnecessary risks. Too many risks in her life have already been taken by other people. It seems to me, as I look around, that she's handling herself pretty well in the circumstances. It isn't always easy to keep your balance out here at the best of times but Katie, without a whole lot of help, is managing just fine . . .

So I tell myself, as I take my leave and promise to keep in touch. I can't honestly say that I've learned a lot about C. though. I'm beginning to feel as if the more I know, the less I understand.

That night I went back to C.'s material on Paradise. The compromise propounded by St Augustine on Adam and Eve and the nature of Original Sin was a sombre message, appropriate to the darkest and most troubled period in the history of Western man – that it was easier for a camel to pass through the eye of a needle than for any but the most repentant sinner to enter the kingdom of Heaven. In fixing his eyes upon Paradise, C. had come up against the source of the Christian belief that human kind was inherently evil. Its scriptural basis was St Paul's statement in his Letter to the Romans that the world was evil because of Adam's sin – 'It was through one man that sin entered the world, and through sin death, and thus death pervaded the whole human race, inasmuch as all men have sinned.' Nowhere does St Paul argue that man by his actions *cannot* avoid sinning, even though God holds him responsible for those actions. Nevertheless the Church Fathers, culminating with Augustine, interpreted him as meaning that mankind is essentially evil and predestined to sin – and this remains Christian doctrine to the present day.

A biographer of Paul, Michael Grant, puts this emphasis on evil into historical perspective. Paul was a Jew with close ties to his compatriots in Palestine who were living, during the first century AD, under the worst provincial government to be found anywhere in the Roman Empire. Downtrodden and persecuted, they felt, just as their ancestors had felt a thousand years before, that they were suffering for the sins of previous generations ... in other words, that their misfortunes were predestined and that evil was thrust upon them. Out of this local, historical circumstance emerged a doctrine of Original Sin, mandated by St Augustine and embroidered by Luther, which still has a quite extraordinary influence on the consciousness of Western man.

There was something about all this which I recognized and which began to explain C.'s preoccupation with Paradise. A mist was beginning to lift, to reveal the shapes and images of a childhood long-forgotten or else long put out of mind.

Aged eight, C. had left home in Uganda, where his father worked for the Colonial Office, to come to school in England. This was the first shock: to be sent eight thousand miles away from his beloved parents and from his home, basking in the warmth of the African sun, where he would run with his friends barefoot under the frangipani trees, to live with his grandparents in a London suburb. I could see him now: a little lost boy in heavy black shoes and a heavy grey flannel uniform, plodding along cold concrete pavements to a cold concrete school, clutching his packed lunch in a red plastic box. He knew nobody; but he knew that he had to eat up all his lunch because not to do so was to invite his grandparents' reproachful reminder of the fate of the Prodigal Son – *And he would fain have filled his belly with the husks that the swine did eat.*

For the second blow was that his grandparents were Methodists, of a more strict and old-fashioned kind even than his parents were then. The Methodism in which C. was brought up derived directly, via John Wesley and Martin Luther, from the Reformation, which reasserted the teachings of St Augustine and the early Church. It believed, as it still does, in encouraging people to experience a conviction of their personal sinfulness, so that they might be led on to obtain forgiveness of their sins through praying to God.

This conviction of sin wasn't to come intellectually, from reading Scripture, but from divinely inspired insight into one's personal guilt and wrongdoing and the need to be saved. An eight-year-old boy was ideal fodder for the work of salvation. C. was made to understand that there was no such thing as a simple naughtiness or mischief. When he did wrong, it was the expression of an incipient sinfulness. Goodness was doing something you didn't want to do but did anyway out of a sense of duty.

Religion had the force of law. Obedience took the place of love. All C.'s thoughts and deeds were under the stern scrutiny of a beneficent God. He was taught that he had to pray every night for this beneficent Being's forgiveness.

In that mahogany-furnished, mock-Tudor-gabled house, in a silence as deep as the grave, with religious texts and prints hanging above the antimacassars, C. learned a distrust of uninhibitedness even more pronounced than the average Englishman's. He was later to find it echoed in the Christian response to Paradise. Everywhere he went looking for representations of Paradise in Byzantine and early medieval art C. found images of fear, humiliation, impoverishment of the spirit. In the frescoes, tomb-reliefs and illuminated manuscripts of early Christianity it was enough to see two naked figures on either side of a snake-encircled tree to be reminded of the inevitable fate of most of mankind. This one scene, repeated thousands of times in books and stone and stained glass, on the walls of churches and on medieval stages in the Eden-tableau of a mystery play, relayed the awful warning and promise. Man fell from grace through Sin. Only through grace might he stand the remotest chance of salvation.

From the age of Charlemagne until the mid-Renaissance, the Temptation and Fall were never represented without a reference forward to what they now prophesied. Sometimes they appear within a long sequence leading up to the Passion; sometimes contrasted with a portrait of the second Adam; sometimes in a single scene condensing the Fall and the Salvation of man. In miniatures and ivory reliefs, the stricken serpent can be seen writhing around the Cross or lying, coiled and powerless, at its foot. Sometimes the Cross rises from the shaft of the serpent-entwined Tree below; or else it springs out of the corpse of Adam himself who, according to legend, lay buried on Golgotha.

It was a simple message. In exchange for Eden, the chance of a Paradise to come. As it was in the beginning, so it just might be, for ever and ever Amen. Not until the end of the Middle Ages did Adam and Eve show signs of escaping from their treadmill of guilt and redemption. And C. had gone a long way towards understanding, and forgiving, the religious impulse behind a Methodist upbringing which had sealed his heart against God.

He had always carried round with him a vivid memory of a Methodist Church service in Orpington to which his Grandpa took him one rainy Sabbath, wearing the heavy black shoes he wore to school (a different school now, down on the south coast). It wasn't long after his Grandma, Minnie, had passed over. C. knew her as a purse-lipped, beady-eyed disciplinarian, who starched and ironed linen until it prickled, and prided herself on her stilted copperplate hand. Normal human affections she showed only towards a fat, smelly, brown-and-white corgi whom C. had to drag choking along the street twice a day for exercise. But Grandpa wanted now to remind C. of all the things that Minnie had done for him . . . her little kindnesses, her dutiful attention to C.'s well-being. If goodness was doing what you didn't want to do out of a sense of duty, Grandma had been a saint.

The church was a modern building (Grandpa had subscribed for it) with a great, gaunt brick interior, unrelieved by ornamentation except for memorials to the dead. After the long, long sermon and the fervent hymns were over, the congregation filing out, the organ still playing solemn chords that swelled with desolation, Grandpa took C. up and showed him Minnie's memorial plaque.

'Read it out.'

'I am reading it, Grandpa.'

'Let me hear you read it aloud.'

To the organ's funereal strains, C. began reading out the engraved inscription. Such was the dreadful, sentimental sanctimoniousness of the occasion that his voice broke; he burst out crying. His grandfather piously comforted him. Members of the congregation, clutching their prayer-books, nodded gravely at the spectacle of a small boy brought to an understanding of Death. And C. felt his heart burst with loathing for the mawkish Protestant religiosity which had compelled him to tears of guilt and unfelt grief.

*   *   *

Rick – he'd remember C. And he'd have plenty of things to say about that time. Over the weekend I'd been staying with my friend Joe, an American professor of Chinese history at the University of Tokyo, who happened to be on loan to Berkeley for this semester. He'd heard of Rick Wanamaker. At least he thought he had; the name rang a distant bell. He promised to track him down for me. I knew Joe. He was tenacious. If Rick was still in the same field of study, Joe would find him.

Monday morning I went back up the hill to the Berkeley campus. I'd just missed Andrea Rush the last time; I wasn't going to take any chances today. Inside the faculty building classes were in progress. I knew my way. In Andrea's corridor doors were opening, people came and went. In front of her door this time lay a large Alsatian. I could just about imagine Andrea with an Alsatian. It studied me lazily as I knocked once, twice. No answer. I tried the handle. The door was locked.

Down the corridor the Social Ecology office was open for business. I explained myself to a helpful middle-aged man who ushered me next door to speak to the Department secretary. Her name was Margaret. That was almost all she would divulge.

She didn't know where Andrea was, no, unfortunately. Nor when she might be coming in: you see, she had only just got back herself. And yes, she was sure that I was a friend, and that I had come out from London, but it was absolutely forbidden to give out home telephone numbers, she was sure I would understand. If I would leave a number where I was going to be for the next few days, she would let Andrea know that I'd called.

I retreated from her stony glare into the outer office. The man on the desk sent me up the other end of the corridor to call on the Head of Department, Carolyn Marchant. Altogether more hospitable, she told me two things. The first was that Andrea had been getting threatening letters through the post, and Margaret was understandably wary of strangers. The second was that on Friday, one week from today, she was off to Africa for three months.

I was desperate. I looked desperate. Carolyn Marchant took pity on me. She gave me Andrea's home telephone number, which I instantly scribbled down. Then she said,

'You know somewhere you might try? The Ariel Café on Shattuck and Cedar. She often stops off there for coffee, mid-morning, after dropping Oliver off at school.'

'Oliver?'

'Yes, Oliver. That's her seven-year-old son.'

*   *   *

Out of San Francisco I took Highway 101 south past San
Jose. I had waited in the Ariel Café from 10.45 until noon,
drinking five cups of good cappuccino. No Andrea. There
was no point in hanging around. I'd left a message on her
home phone, and headed south. I still had time. I cut back
towards the coast on 17 through Los Gatos, up through the
wooded mountains and the old mining communities, before
dropping down to Santa Cruz.

I knew this route of old; surprisingly little had changed.
Thirteen years of commercial development in the fastest-
growing state in the Union hadn't succeeded in eroding the
grandeur and dignity of these coastal mountains, or made
the well-bred little townships within them any less conscious
of their solitariness. In Santa Cruz I booked into a
TraveLodge, had a shower, checked there were no messages
and headed up towards the University.

There were still five people I had to find, from the summer
of '76. All they had in common, apart from the house itself,
was the key which would unlock the past. Besides, I was
curious about UCSC. It had been a community so much of
its time, the idealistic sixties and seventies; I wanted to see
how it had fared after two terms of President Reagan.

The University of California, Santa Cruz, was established
in the mid-1960s as an act of faith in the idea of a liberal
education. Almost everywhere else in the United States
corporate capitalism had come to dominate the institutions
of higher education, demanding that courses be specialized
and geared to business interests. Universities had become
fragmented into specialized schools and research units, all
of them competing for grants by turning out graduates who
could move smoothly into business, industry and the profes-
sions without needing a whole lot of expensive training.

The consequence was that by the 1960s a campus such as Berkeley had become almost indistinguishable from a business college – glamorous and prestigious, but also bureaucratic, impersonal, dehumanizing.

The founders of UCSC – Clark Kerr, Dean McHenry and Page Smith – set out deliberately to turn the tide, or at any rate to build a breakwater against the encroaching commercialization of US campuses. They determined to build the kind of university which would be proof against business pressures and would provide the kind of broad education in the humanities which had served America so well since the days of Jefferson ... the liberal education from which had sprung the nation's greatest thinkers and writers, statesmen and entrepreneurs. As Kerr and McHenry saw it, UCSC would light a beacon from its hill-top above Santa Cruz which would beckon students from across the United States. It would serve as a model for higher education in its best and purest form, and would forestall the closing of the American mind.

Arriving at UCSC in the spring of 1976, C. saw nothing extraordinary about its layout: the colleges, each so different and challenging in their architecture, scattered across the wooded hillside in the afternoon sun. He had been to Cambridge University; he was used to the collegiate system; he felt at home in it. But to American students, many of whom had travelled across America to this beacon on a hill, UCSC came as a profound shock – sometimes so much of a shock that they were never able to reconcile themselves to the place.

It was a simple matter of organization. By borrowing from the traditional British college system, and having every undergraduate discipline taught within the college instead of in separate empire-building departments, the founders sought to stave off the Berkeley syndrome. This way meant that undergraduates could have close rapport with their teachers, and that they could live among people studying every subject on the curriculum. They would develop a breadth of acquaintance which would stretch their intellectual horizons.

How quixotic this idea must have sounded at the time to the big battalions! But it seemed to work. As it became widely known in schools across America that UCSC had developed a curriculum and a teaching system which actually put undergraduates first – instead of subordinating them to the individual and competing interests of faculty staff – students and teachers flocked to Santa Cruz. Once there, the students became part of a small, efficient community set up to take care of their needs. They were taught by college-based faculty, within the college, and could enjoy college activities as well as the facilities of the University as a whole.

The system as I say worked well – too well, really. Despite opening a new college every year, UCSC was able to accommodate less than twenty per cent of qualified students applying to come. Those lucky enough to get places found themselves part of a high-powered yet flexible enterprise offering a wide variety of courses and the opportunity for independent research under the guidance of some of the best professors in the USA. Cowell, the 'arts' college to which C. was affiliated in 1976, boasted on its college staff not only the world-famous Freudian cultural critic Norman O. Brown (one of the gurus of sexual liberation in the 1960s after his book *Life Against Death* argued that psychoanalysis alone offered hope for the regeneration of the senses) but also Harry Berger, on loan from Yale where he had already made an international reputation as a cultural philosopher.

For all that, there was something about UCSC that C. had mistrusted. Walking up to the central administrative building, after an absence of thirteen years, I experienced the same mingled feelings of admiration and alarm. Someone directed me to the Registry. Term had only just started; the counter was busy with unexpectedly young students in sandals, pigtails and muslin shirts, organizing their semesters. I waited my turn, then asked a smartly dressed woman in winged spectacles where alumni records were held. She looked at me in astonishment.

'Did you say 1976?'

'Yes, that's right.'

'You were here in 1976. Let's see, that's thirteen years ago.' Her spectacles dropped and dangled on her bosom, held by thin silver chains. 'Well, young man, I'm really not sure we can help you. I don't think our records go back that far.'

She was making out like I'd said 1876, as though I were a ghostly revenant from some dim and distant period of history. Except that, according to Webster's *Dictionary*, history is a record of past events. If UCSC had no records, I and the others at Topside weren't even history. We didn't exist.

Dumbfounded, I stared at her. Winged Spectacles softened a little.

'What are the names?'

'Well one was called Rick Wanamaker. He was studying and teaching Chinese History. History or Political Science. Then there were two undergraduate students, Helen and Jan. I'm afraid I don't recall their surnames but I thought maybe class-lists —'

'We couldn't help you on the undergraduates even if you knew their full names,' she interrupted firmly. 'We don't keep records of undergraduate students from the mid-seventies. You'll have to try elsewhere for them. The graduate student . . .' she wrote down his name. 'Rick Wanamaker. Let me see what I can come up with.'

She bustled away. I waited, leaning across the counter like a private detective down on his luck. Winged Spectacles returned, looking pleased with herself.

'There *was* an R. Wanamaker doing postgraduate research here for a while,' she confirmed. 'I've checked with Academic Records; he left to go to the University of Wisconsin, Madison. Though he may have moved on: that was some time ago.'

'Oh.'

'Come back to us if you have any problems. Have a nice day now.'

I thanked her and walked slowly back to the car. I was progressing. I knew (or thought I knew) where to find Andrea. I was on the trail of Rick. Howard had given me a telephone number for Lowrie Fredericks. That left from Spring Street, Hélène, Jan and Howard's other live-in girlfriend Rose Seeger ('somewhere in the Los Angeles area') to locate. So, fine. But the fact remained that out of the seven people I wanted to talk to I had so far met up with only Howard and Katie.

There was time yet. I would come back, if necessary; I knew I wouldn't give up. I'd go back to the house on the hill to see if Phil-the-landlord could give me any leads. And I'd ring the University of Wisconsin from the TraveLodge, and I'd go to see Lowrie Fredericks while I was in Santa Cruz and test her memory of 1976. It was time to get moving. Disposing of a pine-cone which had somehow got lodged under the brake-pedal, I headed away from the campus, leaving behind only a hint of carbon monoxide on the Arcadian breeze.

This time I couldn't help but observe Spring Street through Howard's eyes. Turning down the driveway from the street I pictured again the old horse corral, nails sprung in the fencing. Oaks stood all round the battered wooden stable. Horses grazed in its shade, or flared their nostrils at the fragrances blowing from the wide pastureland which soared up to heaven on the far side of the driveway. The picture faded. Where there had been the scuffing of hooves, now there was the hum of an electric lawnmower walked by a man in a cowboy hat and bermuda shorts up, down and around the wooden picnic-table at the end of a flagstone path laid out from the back door of his new farm-shingled homestead.

Further down the driveway, past the two new houses, a rusting chassis squatted in a path of weeds. Then Topside. The house, white and pretty, was unchanged from Howard's day; no way of surmising the emptiness inside. The garage, straight ahead, was a different matter. On my first visit, a week ago, I hadn't noticed the litter of cardboard boxes and old sofas, the rusting car; and outside the garage a sprawl of dustbins, some on their side with logs to hold them down, and more stuff covered in black plastic sheeting at the rear. My old landlord would have kicked ass over that.

I rang the bell, and waited. It was going on late afternoon. Classes on campus would surely have finished. But, once again, nobody answered; nobody came. I gazed round. On the other side of the driveway was the wooden stile leading straight over into the meadowland.

I vaulted over, and at once I caught the breath of a sea wind on my face, and the sky suddenly opened up all around me, cloudless and blue as Jacob's-ladder. The late spring grass, short and springy under my feet, was already the colour of lion's skin. Grass and sky, and along to my right a spear of dark green live-oak camouflaging a scarp of plunging hillside.

How well I knew this landscape, its gentle, hard-edged beauty. I had known it all my life: not just from that earlier summer in Spring Street but from a childhood spent in East Africa on the high grasslands. For any European raised under those giddying skies and extravagant horizons, a journey to America is like returning home. The infinite possibilities of childhood are rediscovered in the expansiveness of the West, its spaciousness of air and light. All at once it made perfect sense that Scott Fitzgerald should have described America as a land commensurate with one's sense of wonder.

Traditionally the English have been wary of the great continental land-masses. The Pilgrim Fathers in 1620 had no burning desire to explore the vulgar immensity of their new-found land. They clambered thankfully on to the Eastern seaboard and stayed put. Not until the end of the eighteenth century did descendants of the *Mayflower* in any number turn their backs on Europe and the sea and venture westwards. But for me all this was like a return to my beginnings in Africa, running barefoot under the milky jacaranda trees and embarking on safari with my parents across great earthen plains where the banks of cloud on the shimmering horizon metamorphosed into stupendous mountain ranges as we drove closer. 'A man's life-work,' wrote Albert Camus, 'is no more than a long journey to find again, by all the detours of art, the two or three powerful images on which his whole being opened for the first time.' I thought about this as I climbed the lion-coloured meadow towards the sky. My child's soul opened on such panoramas.

The scrub-filled arroyos, like the prongs of a pitchfork, were pushing me higher up the hill towards the boundaries of UCSC. Campus Drive was invisible over to the left, but I had come out on to the old wagon-road which ran parallel to it all the way to Fenton. Hardly more than a track in the grass now, this was one of the ancient coast-trails up California. In its time it had been a post-road and a fire-road, and a route down to the cement kilns from the lime-workings in the hills. Generations of ranchers had been this way on horseback and then by pick-up truck. Now it lay abandoned, a track used by the occasional jogger who ploughed up the hill without a second glance at the two sawn-off redwood trunks like telephone poles which stood each displaying a sign in red lettering on weather-beaten tin. *Posted. Keep out.* And *Posted. No Trespassing.*

I stopped here, as C. had done once before, thirteen years ago, with Laura. It was the first time he had taken her across the stile and into the meadowland he had made his own. Talking about his Paradise book and the myth of Eden – was it really about irrecoverable loss, or did it hold out hope for a still-attainable perfectibility? – they had arrived at this point and laughed at themselves. Holding hands, they laughed at what they saw was an omen of good fortune, because they knew that the way into Eden wasn't barred for them. They knew that they were headed there, and that a couple of rusted signs on posts beside an old wagon-trail weren't going to stand in their way.

Laura – I have to tell you something about Laura now. She was a part of that summer I didn't wish to dwell upon – not until I had managed to see her and learn her side of the story. I've said that C.'s quest for Paradise was associated with a dream of fair women; more than anything else that happened in Spring Street, Laura was the reason for my being here today; I didn't want to rush it and get it wrong. But once I had climbed over the stile it was too late for mental evasions. I had to be honest with myself and admit that this was no casual, impromptu walk through the meadows. It was a pilgrimage.

I had come out here because I wanted to know if the places C. had been with her were still as I remembered them. How many times had C. walked up here by himself before he knew Laura? Enough times to discover places of extraordinary beauty and solitude in these hills, and to know that the most personal thing he could share with Laura was his feelings about them. In a kind of exhilaration he had explored the pastureland and the arroyos and given names to the discoveries he made in his private paradise, like Adam naming the first animals.

At the end of one of the wide promontories of grass stretching out levelly between the arroyos he had chanced upon a sheep-path, which twisted down into a ravine. He followed it as it tunnelled under a canopy of thick live-oak with spiny leaves. The ravine widened, and suddenly he was standing in a cwm, or cirque, hollowed out of the side of the canyon. Ivy-covered cliffs rose on three sides. Following the track further he arrived at a small stream on the valley floor and a grassy clearing where ropes of sunlight penetrated through the trees.

He could see no cigarette-wrappers, cartridge-cases, aluminium cans; none of the detritus of civilization. Nobody had been here. He was alone. Magically, gracefully, the place composed itself for him in all its particulars – the sunlight, the trickling stream, the patch of grass, the birdsong, the cradling cliffs – in the way that, standing by himself in a deserted art gallery, he had seen a great painting compose itself in front of him as if it had waited for this moment of communion to surrender the quintessence of itself.

C. retraced his steps the following day to make quite sure that he hadn't imagined it. This time he was struck, not just by the solitary beauty of the clearing but by the eerily sacral approach to it: down the twisting path hidden in the trees, through the narrow tunnel of scrub, and out into the natural amphitheatre brooding in green darkness over the bright secret on the valley floor. It was like a sign – it *was* a sign – that the spirits of place, the green gods of California, had conferred their gift upon a stranger. Less than half a mile from Santa Cruz, two miles from the crowded Boardwalk, they had granted C. admittance to a hidden sanctuary where no one came.

The Path. The Tunnel. The Amphitheatre. The Sanctuary. C. christened them and kept them to himself, until Laura came into his life. Then he escorted her, with all the sense of occasion of Virgil escorting Dante through the Ravenna pinewoods, down the canyon to his sunlit clearing. He knew the green gods would not object. She was, far more than him, a child of theirs; and it was the springtime of the year. Without demur it became part of the two of them, part of their history.

Which was why I could not now resist going back.

First I had to locate the path. All these canyons looked the same, roofed over by scrub oak which concealed their contours. I skirted the nearest one carefully – no way in there. Crossing the first promontory, creamcups sprinkled in the grass, I found a narrow path which seemed to lead into the next canyon; but it soon disappeared completely under a tangle of live-oak and blue elder. I struggled onwards, trying to keep my balance above the precipices.

This couldn't be right – the hostility! I'd never had to fight through undergrowth so fierce. Leaves and thorns scratched my hands. What was I doing down here? A forty-year-old Englishman stumbling blindly through a Californian arroyo looking for something left behind half a generation ago. With scratched skin and scarecrow hair I eventually struggled back up to the top and stepped out into the late afternoon, panting like a fugitive.

One more arroyo lay ahead. Then I'd call it a day. I crossed the next grassy promontory. Dry leaves crackled underfoot. Here, at the end, was a path of sorts. I burrowed down it like a treasure-hunter. It broadened, the way I remembered. Live-oak, holly-leaved, bent branches in a dark arcade over my head. The path twisted downward – then it stopped.

Plumb across it was a tall iron gate, closed and bolted. Barbed wire was stretched either side of it into the thickets. The ground beyond had been cleared. On the other side of the gate the path went on downhill, but unrecognizably. Down ahead in the valley were factories . . . what looked like gas tanks . . . and a parking lot, with the outskirts of Santa Cruz on the far side of it. Sunlight flashed off a wing-mirror.

I stood and gazed through the bars of the gate. Then I

turned round and climbed back up the hill. I must have made a mistake. I must have got the wrong path. Besides, it was getting late. From where I stood I could see Topside, its white chimney and maroon-shingled roof. I set a brisk pace back, past the sign that said *No Trespassing*, and clambered over the stile.

The door into the yard was open. I walked through. No one was around, not even the fat girl sunning herself under the lemon tree. For the purposes of record I took out my camera. I photographed the gaudy nasturtiums growing out of the flyblown dung-heap which used to be Howard's vegetable garden. I photographed the pine-shaded point that was now bulldozed like a building-site. *I mean, the garden was fabulous*, I could hear Howard saying. *It went all the way out to the point, and there were exotic plants, and pipes on top of the fences which came down and watered them all* . . .

Although the back door was open on to the patio, I no longer wanted to enter the house. How could I have imagined for a moment that any of its floating population would have heard of Hélène, or Jan, or know where to find them? In this country, with its ceaseless growing and pressing forward, there was room for everything except the past. Moving on ceaselessly, people out here travelled light, and left their memories behind like so much unwanted luggage in an empty room. And if one day you wanted to reclaim it, and look around at half-forgotten scenes, chances were that the way would be barred and a *Keep Out* sign posted, and you'd know that whatever lay on the other side was beyond restitution.

*　　　　　*　　　　　*

Beep . . . beep.

'*Hallo. Is that the Office of Social Ecology?*'

'*Yes.*'

'*May I please speak to Dr Andrea Rush?*'

'*She's not here. Sorry.*'

'*I've left messages on her phone but I've been moving around a lot. Will she be in later?*'

'*I don't know, sorry.*'

'*Am I speaking to Margaret?*'

Silence. Then, '*Who is this?*'

'*I thought so. Can you please tell her that it's Christopher Hudson still trying to contact her, and that I'm at the TraveLodge in Santa Cruz?*'

'*Sure.*'

Click.

*   *   *

It wasn't altogether true, about moving on and leaving memories behind like unwanted luggage. Lowrie Fredericks had moved on a little way – about five miles to be exact, to a single-storey frame house in a quiet suburban street in Aptos. But I got the impression, as soon as we met and started talking, that the luggage of the past, specifically of her time in Spring Street, was piled up all around her and much as she wanted to kick it away, she hadn't been able to.

We were sitting outdoors drinking Zinfandel in a shopping mall, on a restaurant terrace overlooking a neat planting of evergreens and a car park. The food passed for oriental: we dunked squares of orange-batter fish into bowls of saffron-tinted rice. Hospitable and friendly, she had greeted me at her front door without the least surprise, like a neighbour calling round to borrow some sugar instead of a visitor from England whom she hadn't clapped eyes on in thirteen years. *Hi. Good to see you again. Sure I remember. Come in.*

Rangier, and thinner in the face, she was still undeniably Howard's first girlfriend during my stay at Topside. Howard had told me that she had changed out of all recognition – not so much physically as in her interests and motivations. I wasn't sure that I'd be able to tell. I had never got to know Lowrie well. Looking at her now, across the fish teriyaki and the little fingerbowls of soy sauce, I wondered what Howard meant.

'Do you ever go back there? To Spring Street?'

'Oh, sure! Well no, not recently, not since Tessa and Tom went away. You remember Tessa and Tom?'

I shook my head. 'They must have arrived after I left.'

'Well, I still see Tessa and Tom, they're about my main friends from back then. They were very supportive, you know, after Howard and I split up.'

'What about Hélène, and Jan? They were living in the house then.'

'Sure, I remember.' Lowrie looked puzzled, then she brightened. 'Hélène was just a kid. Very friendly. A bit difficult, wasn't she? She used to drive a beat-up little orange Datsun. Jan – she was nice, real nice. I kinda don't recall . . .'

'They used to garden with you, in Howard's vegetable garden and along the terrace. It was very hot –'

Lowrie smiled. 'That was a full-time job, keeping that vegetation at bay. And the poison oak. Rick used to garden.'

I nodded.

'He was there, you remember? Dark. Kind of Jewish. A scruffy beard. And Andrea. I remember Andrea best of all. Marxist-feminist-Lesbian she called herself. She was so ... theatrical. I remember once we were sitting in the dining-room with some people from outside, and it was very hot? And Andrea, she just got up and removed her blouse – she wasn't wearing anything underneath – and she sat down just like that and carried on talking!'

I looked at Lowrie. There had to be some amnesia here. 'She wasn't the only one to go around like that. I seem to remember, didn't you –'

Lowrie was nodding. 'She was real impressive, Andrea. She lived in a camper, you know? When she first arrived? Then she moved into that suite of rooms at the end.' She looked at me directly. 'You say you got my address from Howard?'

'Yes.'

'How is he?'

'Fine. He's married to Tessa. Another Tessa.'

'Oh yes.'

'I mean, you know, he split up with Rose Seeger a long time ago.'

Lowrie pushed her plate away. 'You were there when that was going on?'

'Yes.'

'Okay. I was ... that was a real bad time for me. My grandmother was dying. I had my graduation that semester. She kind of took over. I started finding her clothes in my closet. Really! Howard said, he just said I had to think about what I was going to do. He wanted Rose living there with him, that's what he was doing and I had to decide what I was going to do.'

Katie had spoken of constant shouting-matches in the annexe; she'd moved out in disgust. Rapt in his private paradise C. had noticed none of it. I said, 'You moved out into the main house?'

Lowrie laughed, without humour. 'I had nowhere to go. I went on living there for a little while, but it didn't work out. I guess I found it pretty hard to forgive Howard for that. The thing about him, well you know, he can be a real neat guy. He's got enormous ... *charisma* in my opinion. I've forgiven him, more or less, I suppose. Although friends of mine, a lot of people, have said to me that I shouldn't forgive him . . .'

She sighed. I thought of what Howard had said to me, that Lowrie was still living in the past, living in Spring Street. After all this time it still hurt, and went on hurting. She hadn't married. She didn't have children. That summer thirteen years ago, so blissful for me, had clouded her life.

'What happened?' I asked.

'That was it, I guess. I got my degree. I went and worked as a research chemist at a big place in Redding, right up north. But I missed my friends in Santa Cruz, so I came back. And now I've met this real nice guy.'

'You have?'

'David. A real nice man. We're going to get married, I think.'

'That's great!'

'Yeah, I think so.' She seemed uncertain. 'He was at UCSC; he graduated the same time I did. He's a fireman now, right here in Aptos. He wants me to become a firewoman, that might be neat, huh? Hey, what's the time?'

It was a quarter to three. Lowrie Fredericks smiled apologetically. 'I'm real sorry, I have to go home and change,' she said. 'My shift starts at four, you see.'

She was a cocktail waitress. That was Lowrie's job now. She commuted to work at Chaminade, a night-club north of Aptos, between Soquel and Santa Cruz. Five nights a week she worked through till the early hours, stuffing the tips into her bra. She'd been there a long time, and served the best tables, and the money was good. You didn't need a qualification in biology, for sure, but Lowrie's university years weren't wasted because she'd certainly learned a lot about men.

The bill came. As we were leaving, Lowrie said – 'About Topside, you asked if I ever went back there? You know I did go back there the other day, just the other day, to look at it. And I thought – it's so small! It's like we were *children* in those days. Everything looked bigger then.'

I asked her if she had any photographs of Topside from that time. An unexpectedly dry smile flitted across Lowrie's face.

'I used to,' she said. 'Not any more. Rose tore some of them up. I guess I tore up the rest.'

*   *   *

In Victorian England, the Reverend Tobias Snowdon won himself a considerable following after he published a book proving that the sun was Hell and that the dark spots on it were gatherings of damned souls. Los Angeles is analogous to this. It has a magnetic attraction; it broadcasts its light across the surface of the earth at twenty-four frames a second; and yet its dark spots of damned souls spread the length and breadth of it, from Burbank across the Hollywood Hills and into East LA. I found it hard to imagine Laura in this company. She fitted into another world, and another time, which were incomplete without her. I was afraid whom I might find. I was afraid whom she might find.

UCSC had located her for me, teaching comparative literature at the University of California, Los Angeles. I had rung her office. Laura had come on to the phone straightaway, her voice amused, diffident, questioning – unchangeable. It was easiest, we both knew then and there, to limit ourselves to practical details about a rendezvous. It didn't take long. Before putting the phone down, she said, after a pause, 'Christopher? I'd just like to thank you, you know.'

'Thank me? What for?'

'When Robert was doing his best to drag me down. I would never have got away if it hadn't been for you. You gave me back my self-esteem, really. You made me feel I was worth something again.'

I had rather thought, looking back, that C. had made life harder for her, not easier, that summer. Robert – let's call him simply that – had been there the day Laura and C. first met, in a bar down on Harvey Estate where a group of graduate students used to meet for Happy Hour. Robert was holding forth to a bunch of people about the influence of Greek culture in fourteenth-century Florence. C. was to hear more than enough about the Classical revival in the months ahead: but for the moment he was transfixed by the slender, green-eyed girl sitting on a table and talking quietly to three or four men gathered round her. This was Laura. She had long, dark, curly hair drawn back from her forehead, and high Red Indian cheekbones (C. turned out to be right about the Red Indian blood) and her voice was musical.

At that time she was living a few miles east of Spring Street, in Soquel, with Robert. That's to say, Robert had moved in to her apartment. A tall New Zealander with thick reddish hair and a pale skin, he gestured and argued with a fierce intensity more familiar in Chicago than in Santa Cruz. He was completely bound up in himself and in what he had to express. That was probably what had attracted Laura in the first place, a kind of mad, self-centred, Van Gogh quality about the man.

But Robert was Van Gogh without the paint brush. *He could not get the words down.* He had trawled most of the major art libraries in the United States and Western Europe, researching his doctoral thesis. He had amassed boxes of documents and notes. He knew his subject in minute detail, and now he discovered that the bigger picture was beyond his ken. The sheer weight of his knowledge bore down on him and encumbered his efforts to turn it into words on paper.

In this predicament Robert had nowhere to turn and no one to turn to, except Laura. She suffered through his tantrums; she took his aching head in her arms and stroked the demons away. She was locked into his waking nightmare, at one and the same time the cause of his afflictions, as he saw it, and the only release from them. He loved her with a terrible hatred. His jealousy and fury were such that Laura, strong-minded though she was, had begun to feel that she deserved them.

At first C. didn't understand any of this. He didn't have a clue what he was getting in to. All he knew was that a clever, beautiful, unpredictable woman had moved into the foreground of his waking vision and everybody else in sight had suddenly retreated to the wings.

Without exactly tracking her footsteps, C. made sure he knew where she was going to be. Her teaching job, that semester, was to give a grounding in the novels of Virginia Woolf to Santa Cruz undergraduates. Most of them had never been to Europe. They knew Virginia Woolf as the person nobody was supposed to be afraid of in the Burton-Taylor movie. Laura ran her hand through her curls in mock despair as she described her attempts to make them grasp the ungraspable. Then she would look at her watch, drain her coffee and pick up her shoulder-bag: she had to go meet Robert.

Bit by bit she told C. about the ordeal she was going through. Hearing all this added to his sense of mission. C. was eager to be a knight-errant riding to the rescue: except that Laura didn't exactly fit his image of the maiden in distress, she was too intelligent and self-reliant. But as luck would have it C. must have met some need in her life, too. He was English; she felt an affinity with that. Unlike Robert, he wasn't a career academic immersed in a doctoral thesis. Unlike Robert, C. had lived in the cosmopolitan world, and one day he would be going back to it.

He met Laura for coffee, a drink, a meal. They met in town, and walked along the pier. C. played his ace and brought her to Topside, and watched her open to its space and light, its flowers and birdsong – what she spoke of as the Englishness of the place. As if sensing it, Howard and the others were instantly at ease with her. C. watched her, all the time, and marvelled at how graceful she was in her movements; she made everybody around her look out of step. And what he marvelled at most was that the grace came from within. Being with her filled him with simplicity.

Looking back, I see that this was when the change in C. began. He had shifted gear on the journey from Chicago, but the Anglo-Saxon scepticism was still lurking somewhere deep down, ready to filter out the chlorophyll. During those first few weeks in Santa Cruz, for all the joy of coming westwards, he couldn't somehow escape the impression of a Disneyland Garden of Eden in which the spellbinding effects were worked by hidden machinery. People out here in California, he decided, had been regressed by Nature to the condition of little children. All their needs were catered for. The sun painted Day-Glo tints on the scenery. Fruit fell off the trees. Waves curled on to long sandy beaches at the right height and spin to make the surfers' day. Gas was cheap. Food and wine were cheap. Life was not to think about; life was to enjoy.

No coincidence was it that the good friends C. made on campus in those first few weeks were both transplanted New Yorkers, Mary and Neil. They were funny, down-to-earth, quick-witted, and they weren't buying. C. liked that Eastern sharpness. They knew that there was a past and a future as well as a present; they knew that somewhere down the line you had to fold your wings and make a landing. Like him, they'd booked their seats near an exit and come along to California for the ride.

C. talked to Laura about this. She had come back to Topside after classes, a jacket thrown over her slim shoulders, and they were sitting on the sun-terrace gazing out over the idiotically beautiful view. To her mind, scepticism was just another word for emotional withdrawal, a way of closing down experience. Things were what we made them, weren't they? She directed a quizzical smile at C. which he recognized as meaning – either you're dumb or you're having me on, and you're not dumb . . . are you?

'I mean, I thought what you were saying about Paradise, in that chapter you showed me, was that it's all to do with the way you look at things. I'm sure that's why you chose to write about Paradise, really, because you thought that's what you were going to find out.'

'I didn't know what I was going to find out.'

'But you believe in it! Don't kid yourself!' She was laughing. 'Why else would you do all this work?'

Dusk was draining the colours away. Laura and C. walked down the stone steps into the garden, and up to the pine-shadowed promontory. Miniature rooms were lighting up on the far side of the canyon. They wandered on, towards the point. Things dropped away on either side. Floating in the darkness they put their arms round each other. They kissed.

Years later when they stepped back, a million stars were out. Laura's eyes were bright and very tranquil. They kissed again, holding each other close. The trees brushed the air; they were enfolded in a dark light. Laura was luminous. They walked back to the house, hand in hand. From a small apartment in Soquel rose a cry of rage and burning frustration, but they didn't hear it, not for a long time, and by the time they did, it was too late.

C. was in love. And being in love opened his eyes to aspects of the Christian Paradise he'd only intellectually perceived before, which were about to transform his study of it. It is all very well for me in retrospect to have made connections between the teachings of the Church Fathers and the joyless Methodism of C.'s upbringing. He himself had never sufficiently questioned what his motives were, until now, for choosing the subject, other than intellectual curiosity. Now he began to understand the profound resentment and anger he felt towards probably the most effective system of moral repression that has ever been instituted in the West. It had affected his entire life, to this point, and it derived directly from the Church's attitude towards women.

The reign of terror waged for centuries by the Catholic Church against sexual love tends to be underestimated nowadays, at any rate in the emancipated West. But for most of its existence, and in most of its sects and denominations, Christianity has been a religion which is worried – no, terrified – by the idea of sensuality.

Man, St Paul believed, was inherently evil – but what made him so? For St Augustine, struggling against his libido, the answer was obvious. Man's desires were what made him evil; man's appetites, above all his sexual appetites. Augustine's theology laid the groundwork for the Christian conviction that the root of all sin was desire which was not directed towards God. The whole drama of the Temptation and the Fall centred upon wrongful desire: Eve's desire in accepting the fruit of the Tree from Satan, and Adam's desire for Eve which made him careless of God's prohibition.

Adam is let off lightly, at any rate until the Renaissance. Eve shouldered the blame. Once again the formula was taken from St Paul (in point of fact a follower of St Paul, since it was written after his death) in his first Epistle to

Timothy – 'Adam was not deceived, but the woman, being deceived, was in the transgression.'

You can't say plainer than that. And in sculptural friezes, in stained-glass windows, in wall-paintings, in medieval mystery-plays, the message is hammered home: it's all the fault of Eve. Medieval artists nearly always included her in their scenes of the Prohibition. They never stopped to think that Eve had not been created when God warned Adam about the Tree of Knowledge of Good and Evil. Or else they thought it made no difference. Women were the weaker sex and therefore liable to sin. Also, with their beauty and their seductive ways, they took men's minds away from contemplation of the holy. All things of beauty were treacherous, unless, like church ornament, gothic vaulting and other forms of visual prayer, they transported people's thoughts heavenwards. And since, of all the appetites, sexual passion was the most impervious to Reason, it followed that women, the descendants of Eve, represented man's greatest temptation.

Pope Gregory, writing to St Augustine of Canterbury at the end of the sixth century AD, reminded him that the sexual act was guilty, not of itself, but because the desire which led to it was evil. The twelfth-century Italian theologian Peter Lombard, whose digest of Christian doctrine was the standard textbook of Christian theology right up to the Reformation, declared that passionate love of a man's own wife was adultery. St Thomas Aquinas, a century later, also warned against a man showing too great affection to his wife. For Aquinas it wasn't the desire as such which was evil, nor the pleasure in lovemaking, but the submergence of the rational faculty which accompanied sex.

'Beasts are without reason. In this way man becomes, as it were, like them in coition, because he cannot moderate concupiscence,' wrote Aquinas in his *Summa Theologica*, which for Roman Catholics remains the most influential of all attempts to reconcile reason and faith. Aquinas goes on to compare the beastliness of sexuality with the state of innocence of Adam and Eve before the Fall who never let their hearts rule their heads.

For one thousand years, in Christian Europe, the delights of sex scarcely find expression, in literature or in art. Bawdy songs and ballads circulated in *samizdat*. Probably there was a thriving under-the-counter trade in dirty woodcuts, though few if any have survived. In public the sensual imagination of medieval man had to be content with the kind of beauty which concentrated the mind on higher things. The Song of Songs, one of the most beautiful and candid of all erotic poems, was solemnly metamorphosed into a dialogue between Christ and his bride, the Church. The Virgin Mary and the female saints could be depicted with some verisimilitude; they were supposed to be beyond the reach of libidinous fantasy. Because they represented an awful warning Adam and Eve could be depicted (usually in miniature) without arousing lust, so the Church decreed. But Eve was bulb-like, with no breasts or hips, and her face had to be expressionless or else cast down in guilty sorrow.

Adam and Eve were naked, and the naked body was an object of humiliation and shame. Classical sculpture which idealized the naked female body was looked upon with a superstitious horror. The art historian Erwin Panofsky recounts the true story of a Greek statue of Venus excavated in Siena in 1334. It was erected in front of the Palazzo Pubblico and stood, much admired, for twenty-three years.

But the late-medieval fear of nudity and paganism took a grip on the good citizens of Siena. They blamed the statue for their defeat at the hands of the neighbouring Florentines. Storming into the Campo they tore Venus down, dismembered her and buried her limbs in enemy territory.

In medieval paintings of the Annunciation, Adam and Eve can frequently be spotted in the background, the idea being that they are losing through disobedience and pride what Mary is winning back through obedience and humility. Eve is the archetype of the faithless, obstinate, empty-headed vamp. Mary, equally unrealistically, is the archetype of perfect femininity, the pearl above price, the fount of all virtue. Woman was Madonna or she was Magdalen: there was no middle way between saint and sinner. Mostly she was sinner. She was Lilith, the Babylonian vampire, the demon of the night. She was Pandora, who opened the box and let evil out into the world. In the Talmudic tradition, *Eve* was derived from the Aramaic word *hiwya* meaning 'serpent' instead of the Hebrew *hayya* meaning 'living'.

It persisted right through the Middle Ages, this identification of the female sex with guilt, temptation and wickedness. Scholars attribute to Petrarch the invention of romantic love; yet it was Petrarch who, in 1346, had this to say about women in his *De Vita Solitaria*, a panegyric to the simple life. 'Adam, that general parent of the human race, than whom, as long as he was alone, no man was happier, but as soon as he received a companion, none more wretched . . . Alone he lived in peace and joy; with his companion in labour and much sorrow. Alone he had been immortal; as soon as he is joined with woman he becomes mortal. Behold herein a clear and conspicuous token of what posterity may hope from the companionship of women.'

All this would be of academic interest, were it not that the Middle Ages bequeathed their Christian values of renunciation and sexual loathing to modern Europe and America. C. was the direct inheritor of St Paul's deep pessimism, Augustine's self-disgust, Aquinas's contempt for the pleasures of the senses. As a result of his upbringing in the Methodist faith, whose *method* indeed was to apply emotional and psychological pressure upon the individual to appreciate his capacity for sin, C. had not been able to rid himself of the association between sex and guilt – just as the Church fathers had planned.

As far back as he could remember, girls had been represented to him as either saints or sinners. The saints were incapable of any sexual liaison beyond a chaste kiss. To dare even to suggest going further would be to defile their purity. They would quite properly reject him with contempt; worse, they wouldn't reject him at all but be ready to go further – worse because that would mean they weren't saints at all, but sinners, all the more dangerous for having assumed disguise.

There was no point in interceding with Reason to combat these atavistic beliefs. Reason was helpless against prohibitions which were superstitious and irrational in the first place. So it was that C.'s first awkward fumblings were accompanied by a terrible sense of sin. He had never had cause to associate his parents with the act of love. He had no brothers and sisters to let him know it was a normal activity – all he knew, thanks to a pamphlet left in his bedroom when he was fourteen, was that masturbation could cause blindness (where on earth did that cock and bull story spring from?).

However consciously C. rejected the attitude that sex was

dirty, some of this stuck fast to his unconscious, whence it surfaced every time he prepared to enjoy himself in the arms of a woman.

Even later on (C. by this time in his early twenties) God, wearing the white moustaches of his Victorian Methodist Grandpa, looked down disapprovingly on C.'s sexual relations. There were some blissful moments. Nilzete was one of them, perhaps because a Brazilian girl somehow escaped the moral categories engraved on C.'s unconscious. But the physical sense of shame took a long time to fade: with consequences, in the way of humiliation and self-loathing, which would have brought grim satisfaction to the sainted killjoys who first blighted sexual pleasure by calling it evil.

In due course C. drove out the saints who were plaguing him. But he did so only by dint of striking a bargain with his unconscious. He would be able to enjoy lovemaking on condition that it had nothing to do with love. This is where we came in, if you remember? Skimming pebbles across Ullswater? Writing dramas of existentialist alienation? C.'s girlfriend at that time was adorable and complaisant: he could lose himself with her, but always, as it were, with an animal passion. They went to a Greek island, and rutted. They went to Venice, and rutted. Actually they were having tender and mutually satisfying sex, but C. couldn't afford to see it this way. Somewhere in the background was the prohibition, the Methodism, the unspoken reproach of people he loved and respected. And his involuntary detachment, withdrawal – call it what you will – communicated itself to women he might have loved. That relationship broke up, and C. repeated the process with someone else.

Sexual love is a meeting of minds and bodies. C. seemed to be capable of one or the other but not the two together;

he retreated; he held back. Even with his current girlfriend in England, whom he knew for a year before going to America, there was an incompleteness caused by something not fully resolved; a failure to give wholly of himself; an absence of the right kind of faith.

Perhaps there *was* no meaningful Paradise. Certainly the passionless Eden of Adam and Eve was no kind of model to choose. I'm sure it said something about C.'s attitude to Paradise that he set out in the opposite direction to where Eden lay according to St Basil and St Isidore, St This and St That, not to mention Mandeville's *Travels* and the fabulous Prester John. They placed it in the Orient: at the junction of the Tigris and the Euphrates, or on an island in the mouth of the Ganges, or further east in the direction of Japan, or possibly at the top of a high mountain such as Mt Amara in Ethiopia. Certainly not on the West Coast of an unknown continent that was to become America . . .

And yet this was where C. found it, not two months into his Spring Street summer. With Laura there were no more bargains; there was no more holding back. He discovered that love and sexual fulfilment were not incompatible, and that sexuality could hold within it tenderness, friendship and spirituality – virtues which Christianity had ascribed to Mary the saint and withheld from Eve the sinner.

Knowing now what love was, knowing how two hearts could seem to occupy a single soul, he also understood that God had never intended Paradise for an elite of Christians who had spent a lifetime washing out their mouths and their imaginations. Nor was it bound up irrevocably with sin and redemption.

It was time to change direction. He would look into Paradise as a place for lovers, a garden of delights in which there were no prohibitions of any kind. If C. read St Paul now, it was not his denunciations of sinfulness he turned to, but his last Epistles, to the Philippians, which were written in a spirit of tolerance and mellow resignation after a lifetime of struggle:

'*Whatsoever things are true, whatsoever things are honest, whatsoever things are just, whatsoever things are pure, whatsoever things are lovely, whatsoever things are of good report; if there be any virtue, and if there be any praise, think on these things.*'

         *   *   *

Here, in Los Angeles, the past had caught up with me, a fortyish family man suddenly unsure of his motives. I had sat in the coffee-house on the University campus. I had walked with her ghost in the high meadows. I had stood on the bulldozed promontory, haunted by nothing but desolation. Now I'd come to the place where Laura was. Driving up to stay with friends in the hills above Sherman Oaks, four million people were one person, taking her keys out of her jacket to unlock her car, and throwing her shoulder-bag on the seat beside her.

That is what terrified me more than anything: my readiness to imagine Laura exactly as she had been the last time. C. had spent the night with her alone by the lake in the Henry Cowell redwood forest; then they'd gone back to the apartment he was renting from her tutor. They'd showered together, and slept a little, and in the morning they had separated – Laura to go back to Berkeley where she was supervising classes, C. to head east, out of California, towards the rest of his life. I still had at home the Navajo bark painting she'd given him in exchange for his farewell present of a bleached horse's skull he had found on a fence-post at Topside. It portrayed two winged beings swooping over the tops of a redwood forest while others stood on the ground and looked up at them.

Laura since had changed, of necessity. She had got older. She had done a lot of experimenting. And for the last six years (she told me this on the phone) she had been married, happily married, to an educational adviser at present staying in Sacramento. Nowadays, for all I knew, she wore a pair of spectacles on a chain like the woman at the UCSC Registry. For all I knew, she dressed like a fashionable Los Angeleno in a suit, with a gold bracelet on her wrist. Perhaps there were children she left with an in-law before going off to play a round of golf.

I got to the location, two blocks south of Wilshire, only about ten minutes late – and then I couldn't find the restaurant. I cruised up and down, slowly, searching for a whitewashed building with a blue trim, on a minor intersection. There wasn't one. Panic struck. It was already 12.20. It had taken me thirteen years to get here: was I going to miss a simple rendezvous?

I parked the car and began half-walking, half-running down the street, darting glances left and right. A lissome figure about a hundred yards further along the sidewalk turned in my direction. I had left my glasses in the car. All I could make out were blue jeans and a red shirt and a halo of dark hair. Laura's eyesight was better than mine. While I was still trying to look casual she ran up and threw her arms round me.

'Hallo, stranger,' she said.

My mind whirled.

'I'm a bit late,' was all I could find to say.

The Iranian restaurant was in front of us, just as she'd described it. What had made me resist seeing it didn't matter now. Laura was sitting across the table from me. She looked exactly but *exactly* the same – gracile, slim-waisted, small-breasted, with extraordinary wide green eyes which were wider and greener than I remembered . . . no older, no older at all.

'But look at all the grey in my hair!' she exclaimed. 'Not like you. You haven't changed one bit!'

'But I'm so wrinkled. Look at all the lines, here, and here. You haven't got any lines at all!'

Which was true. We laughed together over the discovery of eternal youth; two bygone lovers in a restaurant.

*   *   *

'So you're a married woman.'

'Yes. And you're married to Kirsty?'

'Yes I am.' I told her how good she looked and how happy.

'Do I? Well it's not surprising, it's really nice to see you after all this time! But yes. Sure. Jim and I are very happy.'

Laura told me how they'd met, in the spring of 1982 in a truck-stop on Mission Street in Santa Cruz. Laura was sitting over a cup of coffee, reading a Latin course-book. Then a strongly built, wiry man came in, a trucker she supposed, and sat down opposite her. He wanted to ask her what she was doing reading Latin in a truck-stop. This was Jim, at that time an administrative assistant at UCSC, in Oakes College.

'He was so attractive. Very gentle and ... *normal*, and that was really important to me. I'd spent so long ... you know, Christopher, I was so mixed up by then, I wasn't sure of anything anymore. I needed someone to be confident of a few things, and Jim had that confidence. He'd come through some very hard times.'

They got married six months after the truck-stop. For the next four years they divided their time between Rome, which they loved, and a black college in Mississippi, where Jim was made Dean.

'We stayed there for two years. It wasn't like being in America at all; Mississippi could have been a country in the Third World.'

'I can imagine.'

The food arrived: skewered chicken in a mound of saffron rice. I wasn't hungry: I had all the nourishment I needed just listening. After Mississippi they had come back to California, Laura to finish her doctorate, Jim to help put together Jesse Jackson's educational programme for the 1989 Presidential campaign.

'I started teaching at UCLA at the beginning of this year.' Laura looked up apologetically. 'I'm sorry, this must be so dull for you, Christopher.'

'Dull!'

'Well you've been doing so much! And the books ... Is Kirsty writing too? You've got children, haven't you?'

'One. Rowley. He's six.'

'Have you got a picture you could let me see?'

'Somewhere. It's at home. I'll send one to you.' I prattled on for a bit about Rowley, and fatherhood, and the Ghost-buster gun I'd promised to bring him back from the United States to show off to his schoolfriends. Laura's face clouded a little. I remembered that she'd said, years ago, long before I could have said the same thing, that for her to have a child would be the most fulfilling thing in the world. Sadly, that fulfilment had not been granted her. The likelihood was that she would never conceive. They were going to give it one more year. If nothing worked, she and Jim would adopt a baby. Meanwhile her long commute to UCLA every day from downtown Los Angeles wasn't helping. Nor was the stress of having an imminent deadline for her thesis.

All this while we had steered clear of my reasons for being here. I began almost to hope that Laura had put the past behind her and forgotten the times I remembered. Then it would have been easier to stifle the emotions welling up in me. But no: she hadn't let go of them. She treasured them as much as I did. That became apparent as soon as we went back to talk in her office at the University, and she allowed herself to travel back to Spring Street and the summer of 1976.

Well . . . I have been a writer and a journalist for most of my working life. I had every intention of being professional; I had a book to write. But understand this: I had literally just come away from those places C. had known with Laura, through Laura, in the meadows and on the promontory. I put the tape-recorder down on the seat between us: we were immediately lawyer and client. I picked up a notebook and a pen: we were journalist and interviewee. It was no good. My heart was too full. What had started out in England as a clever idea, what had developed over here into an engrossing exploration of memory, was escaping from my control.

Most of us think of memory as an energizer of our past

life, colouring it and shaping its forms through the process of recollection. Now I found it acting upon the *present* in powerful, unexpected ways. There were tears in my eyes. They were matched by hers, and the colour coming and going in her face. I kept offering to stop, anxious that I was making too many demands upon her. Laura didn't want to stop. There was something ceremonious and formal about the act of remembrance for both of us, as though it represented something beyond itself – a tying-up of loose ends, a peaceful exorcism.

In the years after C. had left California she had been back and back to the places they had shared and in a sense invented. She had revisited the picnic-place in the high meadows, and the clearing that I hadn't been able to find any more. She had stopped by the Gallows, C.'s name (she reminded me) for the twin poles on the old wagon-road, *Posted. No Trespassing.* She had walked along West Cliff, where they had sat side by side watching the Pacific and the surfers loitering in the shallows. She had tracked back into the Henry Cowell redwoods, to the place deep in the forest which on the map is called the Garden of Eden, where they had spent their last night together, bathing in the moonlit river.

She'd been back as well to Harvey Stadium where they'd first met, but the bar had been levelled to make way for a housing development. She had a vivid memory of first setting eyes on C. (actually, on the back of his head) because of the presentiment she felt, as vivid as the first picnic together up in the hills.

'The first picnic?'

'You don't remember?'

'Well yes but ... wasn't it after that time we were together on the promontory, that evening in Spring Street?'

'No. It was before. It was *before*. Don't you remember?' Laura grinned. 'It was a very *full* picnic, I'm surprised you don't remember. You took all that trouble . . . French bread, pâté, cheese, Mondavi wine . . . really I was impressed!'

'Go on.'

'After we finished the picnic you took me down the hill into the trees –'

'Into the canyon.'

'Was it a canyon? I remember going down a path under the trees, and you were giving names to everything, like Adam naming the animals. It was as if nobody had ever been there before. There was a kind of valley –'

'The amphitheatre –'

'Yes. The amphitheatre. And you remember along the bottom of the valley . . .'

'A stream.'

'A little rivulet. You had a name for that, too. And remember, you were standing by a tree and you pulled me into your arms and kissed me. And then you began undoing the buttons on my blouse. And . . . well! I was taken by surprise, I guess. Surprise rather than indignation; I pulled back a little. In fact I stepped back across the stream. Just for a second, then I stepped back over, to you. And you know, it was so strong the impression, I've never forgotten it, so vivid . . . the feeling I had that I'd crossed a Rubicon. I had taken a step which would change my life. And it did.'

We were silent.

When I could speak, I said, 'In that it gave you back courage in dealing with Robert?'

Laura nodded. 'That too.'

Our hands pressed. Footsteps came and went along the

corridor. It wasn't a time for speaking. We both knew that Robert was only a part of it.

*   *   *

The next time that C. and Laura took a picnic into the hills I don't recall they got down as far as the stream. They found a quiet, hidden place to lay the rug down, and took their clothes off and made love. Could be, they didn't bother with the rug. Anyway the next few weeks, until Robert happened upon them, were the nearest to paradise of any time that C. had known in his life.

He had no responsibilities. He was a traveller passing through. It didn't matter what the future might bring. It was enough that he was bringing happiness to a woman he'd fallen in love with, and was gradually making her love him too. That they met in secret, and stole time to be by themselves, added piquancy to the affair, at least in C.'s eyes. He didn't have to go back each night to a jealous, resentful, potentially violent partner who depended on him for peace of mind.

C. offered to have it out with Robert. The idea filled Laura with dread. 'You don't know him, you don't know what he's like!' She caught her breath. 'Please don't let's think of Robert. Please. I'm so happy just to be with you!' And C. would consent manfully, feeling like Lancelot giving Guinevere a new lease of life. For her part, Laura wanted to lose herself in him. There was a loneliness in her. But mostly she wanted to believe in herself again and to feel that she was a woman. She wanted to know that she could be loved for herself: and the most precious thing C. could give her, and did give her, was this knowledge.

They made love on floors, on rugs, on the grass – pretty much everywhere except in bed. Bed was complicated. Robert lurked in her Soquel apartment, and C.'s own bed in the Spring Street alcove was narrow. Besides, Laura seemed superstitious about beds, as if they might domesticate their relationship (as it turned out, she was right to be superstitious about them, though not on that account). She did possess a capacious sleeping-bag, which she brought to Topside for the early afternoons when the rest of the household was up on campus. They laid it on the floor of the living-room and snuggled inside.

One afternoon Rick came home early and wandered in as they were writhing on the floor. C. looked up from the sleeping-bag to find him gazing down.

'Hallo, Rick,' C. said.

'Hi.' He stood and stared, a look of amused curiosity on his face, as if they were peasants in one of the Chinese communes he had been on a field-trip to observe. C. scowled at him.

'Was there something you wanted?'

'Not really. I just wondered if it was anyone I knew.'

Laura poked her head out.

'Oh, fine,' said Rick, and wandered out.

Laura was privileged to have her own carrel, or box-room, in the University library. She gave C. a key. He would slip in there when none of the librarians was looking. On campus it was their meeting-place – sometimes more than that – and it was the only spot in the University where C. had complete privacy to do his work. With a lover's selfishness he appropriated it, more or less, as if he needed to invade her professional as well as her private life. It was full of things he adored: her books, notepads with her neat, black-ink handwriting, odds and ends which had no meaning for C. other than that she had chosen them, which was enough to make them priceless.

He showed her what he had written about the Church's attitude towards carnal desire. Laura frowned and then laughed and said, 'Aren't you forgetting Dante and Beatrice?'

'That's what I'm going on to say. It wasn't real to Dante. He was using their love as a human image of the transcendent love of God, just like his Garden of Eden is an earthbound image of the heavenly paradise ahead. Don't you think?'

'Yes, but without the woman there wouldn't be a *Divine Comedy*. Isn't it the earthly reality of Dante's love for Beatrice on which the whole spiritual structure of the poem is built?' She quoted those beautiful lines from the *Purgatorio* when Dante sees Beatrice again, and Virgil, knowing there is nothing more for him to do, slips away –

> *Then came on me, needing no further sight,*
>   *Just by that strange, outflowing power of hers,*
>   *The old, old love in all its mastering might.*

Dante was part of Laura's doctoral thesis; C. wasn't going to argue with her. And anyway, what mattered the Church's views any longer on guilt and sin? *Felix culpa*: the apple was good for Adam and Eve to eat because it allowed them to enjoy a freedom they would never otherwise have possessed. By refusing the state of servitude and disobeying God, Adam and Eve were able to make the passage from the sensual to the spiritual. Out of the realms of mere animal desire they could come gradually to love, and to develop a taste for beauty – above all, to understand themselves. Had Adam not sinned, Man would have stayed God's creature. As a result of his fortunate fall he was raised on to a higher plane, the adopted son of God, interceded for by the Virgin Mary and by Christ's act of redemption.

Working in Laura's carrel, C. turned his attention to secular parallels to the Garden of Eden – gardens of love whose illicit delights were heightened by association with the primal innocence. The first and most famous, the allegorical Song of Solomon, is neither an allegory nor by King Solomon, but it set the tone. '*A garden inclosed is my sister, my spouse; a spring shut up, a fountain sealed.*' To which the bride replies, '*Awake, O north wind; and come, thou south; blow upon my garden, that the spices thereof may flow out. Let my beloved come into his garden, and eat his pleasant fruits.*'

Probably of Persian origin, the earliest 'paradise' was a royal hunting-park planted with evergreens and fruit-trees. Early stone reliefs have carvings of wild animals in these parks lying down peacefully beneath the trees. A fragment from the Assyrian palace at Kyundjik shows a lion resting on its forepaws beneath vine-branches and lilies.

After the fall of the Roman Empire it was monks who preserved the idea of paradise as a garden. At least from the establishment of the Benedictine order, in the sixth century, there were monastery gardens called paradises. They were originally planted as herb gardens, for medicinal purposes, but since roses and lilies were among flowers accepted to have curative properties, herb gardens were also tended for their beauty. A drawing from the twelfth-century *Hortus Deliciarum* pictures a saintly recluse who has reached the last rung of the ladder of salvation. His mind lingers on the beauty of his earthly garden, and he falls to damnation.

Medieval castle gardens provided pleasures of a more carnal sort, as woodcuts remind us. Safe behind the battlemented wall, sitting on the grass or reclining on the turfed seats between the trees, the nobles talk and sing, play the lyre, gamble and dally amorously with their lovers.

The most famous of all secular gardens in the Middle Ages is that of the *Roman de la Rose*, a French poem of the thirteenth century. What happens, in the first part of the poem written by Guillaume de Lorris, is essentially the story of the Garden of Eden. Passion enslaves the Lover and overthrows Reason. Let into this garden of courtly love by Idleness the gatekeeper, the Lover compares it to the earthly paradise but considers that there is no place in paradise as good to be in as this. Although Jean de Meun, who wrote the later part of the poem, condemns the garden as false compared to the real Christian Paradise, it was de Lorris's garden of Delight, with its delicious rose-bud surrounded by a sweet-smelling hedge at the centre of it, which captured the imaginations of writers for centuries to come.

Dante's earthly paradise is a place of purification. The paradise garden of Guillaume de Lorris is dedicated to sexual fulfilment. But in one respect they are almost identical. Their descriptions of birds, trees, fruit, fountains and soft breezes are borrowed in every particular from the paradises of the classical world. The pagan setting of the earthly paradise remains constant, in Christian art and literature, right up to the Renaissance and beyond.

It has two streams: one epic, one pastoral. The best known of all, in the direct tradition of Homer's Islands of the Blessed at the end of the world, is Virgil's description of Elysium in the sixth book of the *Aeneid*. No classical evocation of the afterlife of the blessed has had a stronger influence on Christian ideas of paradise than the green lawns and joyous scenery which refresh Aeneas, coming up from his sojourn in the Underworld to this place of bliss:

> *Where souls take ease among the Blessed Groves.*
> *Wider expanses of high air endow*
> *Each vista with a wealth of light. Souls here*
> *Possess their own familiar sun and stars.*

None of the later Christian attempts to evoke an earthly or celestial paradise outdoes this in exalted beauty. But Virgil then switches to a description of shady groves, rustling woodland copses, meadows refreshed by streams, and singing and dancing among the immortals, which bears heavily on the other stream of paradise imagery, the pastoral.

This took C. further back still, to the *Idylls* of the Greek poet Theocritus written in the third century BC. Some of the most beautifully crafted poems in any tongue, their setting shaped the familiar Western vision of what a paradise should contain.

In an upland Mediterranean landscape of pines and tamarisks and clear water brimming out of rocky springs, herdsmen sit in the shade, drinking good red wine and conversing. In the seventh *Idyll*, Simichidas and his friend Enkritos celebrate the harvest festival almost literally in the womb of nature. They lie in the shade, on beds of rushes, beside a spring of sacred water, drinking and making music. The larks and thistle-finches sing, the cicadas chatter, pears and apples lie about them in abundance, and all things breathe the scent of summer and ripe fruits.

These ancestors of the pastoral tradition live in a state of give-and-take with nature. Everything is in balance, in harmony, in a self-contained world. Does it sound familiar? As I re-read what C. had written about Theocritus, I began to analyse the uneasiness I had felt again as I drove up to the University of California, Santa Cruz, in its beautiful pastoral setting carved out of ranchland and pine forest. Before I try to explain what I mean, let me take you on a short tour of the domain.

Once through the main entrance, we drive round past several original stone farm buildings – a granary, a barn, a cook-house – austerely preserved in order to convey an impression of continuity. The road winds up through Elysian parkland, higher and higher, offering breathtaking views of Santa Cruz and the Bay as it traverses the hillside. The tall green redwoods enfold us as we swing round towards the first low white college buildings discreetly hidden in landscaped glades – Cowell College, Merrill College, Crown College up on the right, its offices and residences giving out directly on to vanilla-smelling pinewoods and bosky paths among the trees.

We turn left, past the amphitheatre hewn out of old limeworkings, and pass a series of buildings which could have been tree-houses so carefully and sympathetically do they blend in with the sylvan setting. They comprise the social centre of UCSC: the Student Services Building, the Classroom Building, and the Redwood Building itself with the Bay Tree Bookstore and the Whole Earth Restaurant where I'm stopping off for a mug of coffee.

What you see around you is as it was in 1976. Or most of it. The Whole Earth Cookbooks have been re-jacketed as New Age Cookbooks, and developments in refrigerated transport allow the place to stock a comprehensive selection of Third World coffee beans or – for the growing number who reject all stimulants – of freshly squeezed exotic fruit juices.

Nothing could be more refreshing, more tranquil, more lovely. No wonder C.'s contacts in Chicago in 1976 had been unanimous in recommending this campus as the closest he would approach to paradise on earth. Up here on the hill, embowered in redwood groves, the outside world is out of sight and out of mind. So mighty are the tree-trunks that it is like living as small children on the forest floor. Students wander in and out of the washed shadows like so many Oberons and Titanias, Rosalinds and Orlandos, wandering out of the wings of a pastoral comedy. And true enough: if, laughing and talking, they stroll out to the clear horizons of the upland meadows, they will be found sharing the scenery with a bucolic herd of cows grazing near the bicycle path.

The blend of Arcadia and Utopia in this description isn't fanciful. It is the consequence of a deliberate attempt by the founders of the University of California, Santa Cruz, to embody the delights of a classic liberal education. In the Arcadian landscapes of Theocritus and Virgil solemn discussions take place in the fresh air, under shady trees. Grapes are eaten; wine is drunk. A brook runs close by that's cool to the feet. In the background a shepherd's flute can be heard piping a melody to his absent love.

Make the grapes hamburgers, the brook a swimming-pool and the shepherd's pipe an acoustic guitar and you have UCSC, the University of Arcadia. It was entirely consistent with the utopian vision of Clark Kerr and Dean McHenry – not in the loose, modern sense of some impractical, escapist dream, but in the strict original sense of those classical Utopias, beginning with Plato's, which set out to criticize existing society by posing a systematic alternative model to it. The blueprint of UCSC was utopian in that it offered an ideal alternative to the commercial corruption of other university campuses. At the same time it was organized in comprehensive detail by men who intended it to succeed, and who had the richest, most generous and prestigious public university system in the United States to back them in their endeavour.

But – look around. Uniformity, not idiosyncrasy, is the distinguishing feature of this campus-paradise. The students, and their teachers, can't help conforming to the setting they find themselves in, when it should really be the other way round. By the very act of creating a paradise, the founders had sowed the seeds of its corruption. They had acted in the best of faith. Knowingly or not they had taken their cue from the patrician pastoralism of Thomas Jefferson, who wrote that unspoiled landscape 'disseminated the germ of virtue'. But, as C. should have known by then, paradises are too beautiful and restful to encourage prolonged intellectual labour. UCSC was an environment to play in, not to work in. It was *unserious*.

In his *Biographia Literaria* the poet Coleridge has an insight so sharp and simple as to be aphoristic. 'In natural objects,' he writes, 'we feel ourselves, or think of ourselves, only by *likenesses* – among men too often by *differences*. Hence the soothing love-kindling effect of rural nature and the bad passions of human societies.' So strongly did nature dominate artifice, here on campus, that differences and passions were neutralized; every arduous intellectual engagement with the real world was made to seem somehow foolish and irrelevant. As Howard said, it was easy to drift off into oblivion. Numbed by the beauty of the place we were on mental sabbatical in lotus-land.

St Augustine had done his best to convince himself that Adam and Eve managed to combine work with pleasure in the Garden of Eden. For Adam it was not 'painful labour' but an agreeable business of conversing with nature and humbly cooperating with the Divine Gardener (Augustine himself was one of a tiny minority of men in the fourth-century Roman Empire who had never needed to soil his hands with manual labour). John Milton, in his much more realistic Garden in *Paradise Lost*, sets Adam and Eve to work like good practical Puritans who don't let the grass grow under their feet . . . their job is to keep the wilderness beyond from encroaching. At UCSC there was no wilderness beyond. Eden stretched to the horizon; Happy Hour was round the clock.

Did C. know what he was doing? I think he had succumbed to that peculiarly Californian form of Temptation – not lust, nor greed, but the sheer facility of everything. He was in a coma of self-satisfaction, *Annihilating all that's made/To a green thought in a green shade*. Nothing was dark, or difficult, or dangerous. He was in love. He had enough money to get by. He thought he understood what was being revealed to him when the snake crawled out of the undergrowth at Topside and proved to be just another plaything – he was being slipped a message that there was no Satan, no force of evil; the whole business of salvation and damnation was a con.

Looking back at him, I felt uncomfortably like the prophet Amos, trailing the manure of his hill-village through the streets of Bethel and shouting at the Israelites to repent. *Woe to them that are at ease in Zion!*

While immersed in his study of paradise gardens, C. had a visitor. Somebody tried the door of the carrel, then unlocked it and came in. It was Robert. It hadn't occurred to C. that he would have his own key. They stared at each other.

'What are you doing here?' Robert demanded.

C. explained that Laura let him use her carrel to work in. His face darkened. 'She's never let me use it,' he said sulkily. 'Why's she let you?'

'I don't have anywhere of my own at the house I'm living in.'

This appeared to satisfy him. C. took him off for a drink.

'You seem to fit in here,' Robert said gloomily. 'Much better than I do. I don't really know what I'm doing here at all. If it wasn't for Laura I would go back to Europe. She's all that keeps me going. She's magic. An angel.'

'How's your thesis going?' C. asked cruelly.

'Oh, very well. There's a lot still to do, of course. It's pretty much uncharted territory. The main thing is to keep on top of it, keep pushing on.'

He looked wretchedly at me and away. 'Laura said you're only in Santa Cruz for a few months. Is that correct?'

'That's my plan.'

'Lucky man.'

It was after Rick that Laura and C. decided sleeping-bags weren't ideal. C. persuaded her to come down to his bed in the alcove. She wasn't happy about it. Since discovering C. at work in the carrel, Robert had started calling her at work, even on the lobby-phone by where she was teaching. Before, he had stayed and worked in the apartment in Soquel. Now he kept appearing on campus, a tall, freckle-faced, carrot-headed figure with a sad, determined tread. At home in the evening he would bully Laura into accounting for every moment of her day, the better to torment himself with fantasies of her unfaithfulness. Obviously he had decided to add jealousy to the list of complexes bedevilling his work. It filled him with frenzy when he couldn't find the proof he was masochistically probing for.

He didn't have long to wait. One afternoon C. and Laura were in bed in Topside. Laura had phoned to say that she was coming over; a class had been cancelled. The house was empty. The two lovers were naked and somnolent in each other's arms. Robert stomped down the stairs and stood over them.

Laura gasped. C. got up. Robert was bright red and panting.

'I thought so.' He kept saying it. 'I thought so.'

'You – you just come down here –' C. was gabbling, saying the first thing that came into his head. 'Laura . . . let Laura put some clothes on. If you want to talk, let's go in the bathroom.'

C. stalked into the bathroom. Robert followed.

'Listen,' said C., 'I understand how you must feel –'

Robert punched him in the face. C. heard Laura yelling something. He got up off the floor and tested his right eye. It was still there.

He said, 'I hope you feel better now.'

Robert was still breathing heavily. He marched up and down, clenching and unclenching his fists. Through his one good eye, C. could see that, now his first blind anger had subsided, Robert was at a loss to know how to go on, confronted by a naked man in a bathroom. He asked him to pass over his bathrobe which was hanging on the back of the door. Robert brought it over, staring at him.

'You'd better have a flannel or something for your eye,' he said.

C. pulled on the bathrobe. Robert found a flannel and moistened it under the tap. C. nestled it gingerly against his swelling eye. While Laura, in tears, finished dressing, the two men stood around being extremely stiff-upper-lip and polite to one another. Both of them were inspired by the high drama of the occasion into the nearest they ever came to friendship. Laura on the other hand, embarrassed and shocked to the depths of her being, had already worked out that nothing would ever be the same again, and was crying as much for that as for the humiliation.

Robert insisted that she come back with him to Soquel. C. refused to hear of it. While the two of them locked horns, Laura slipped away.

'Where did you go?' I asked her now. Laura had put down her chopsticks. She pushed her plate away with a look of real distress.

'I don't know. It was so *awful*. I can't even think about it.'

It was the following evening. We were in a Japanese restaurant on the other side of the freeway from her home. The place she was staying was an hour's drive south through Los Angeles, in a blue-collar neighbourhood quite close to Knott's Berry Farm. The houses were small and neat, white-painted, standing in square fenced lots either side of the street. Cats uncurled in the orange twilight and licked themselves as I rang the bell. Laura came to the door in slacks and a white T-shirt, and we went off to eat sushi.

She was quiet and a bit withdrawn. In three weeks she

had to hand in her doctoral thesis and she was blurry with fatigue. I saw what I'd been putting her through. I had breezed in on an emotional high from Santa Cruz and I'd expected Laura to meet me on the same emotional level. What I'd failed to consider was that I would be asking her to relive a period of her life which in a lot of ways had been painful. It could be why she had chosen a restaurant called Scheherezade for our first rendezvous – Scheherezade, the girl required by the vengeful Sultan Schariah to tell him story after story after story through the long Arabian nights.

'Awful, yes. But quite comical too, I suppose, in retrospect, me and my black eye.'

'No. It wasn't funny at all.'

She had coloured up at the memory. While Robert and C. had been working out their aggression in a courtship ritual, Laura had been left with no outlet for her feelings of humiliation and guilt. She said,

'It was the worst moment of my life.'

'It didn't stop us seeing each other.'

'Of course not.' She looked at me quizzically and a little sadly.

'I still have that Indian bark painting you gave me,' I told her.

'I still have the horse's skull,' she said.

Back in her rented house, sparsely furnished except with books, Laura showed me photographs of Jim and herself in Rome. We talked a bit more about Spring Street, the people I roomed with. Most of the names had gone: though she remembered getting strong feelings of disapproval from Jan when she moved in on Jan's experiment with me. Howard she remembered with affection. He had behaved towards her with a kind of amused paternalism, as if she helped to confirm his belief in the utopianism of Topside by making me fall in love with her.

Neither of us had spoken for a little while. I checked my watch. It was past midnight.

'I suppose I should let you get to bed,' I said awkwardly. 'I've taken up an awful lot of your time.'

Laura flinched. 'I'm sorry, I don't think I've been very helpful to you.'

Too late I realized that I had wound up our meeting like a professional interviewer, and cursed myself.

'Oh, you have, you have!' I insisted. 'And it's not just . . . about that.'

'I shouldn't have said all that, should I? I've embarrassed you, I went too far.'

'No. No. I wanted you to . . . I wanted *us* to talk like that.'

'Really?'

'Forget the book,' I urged. 'Think of the book as an excuse.'

And Laura was too kind to reply – Why should I? Aren't you planning to put all this in?

There was nothing more to say. Somewhere back there two people had known a sort of Eden, and that had to be an irrecoverable loss. I couldn't tell how much I'd changed, in Laura's eyes. Possibly she was confused about it too: since she was face to face with a man who was more interested in recovering his old self than in revealing the new. But she had nothing of herself to hide. I had gone back in search of the Laura I had known and I'd found her, and she instilled everything around her with significance as she used to do.

She walked me to the car. I embraced her, and felt in my arms the strange, skinny, wild, vulnerable creature C. had embraced on the promontory at Spring Street with the lights going on and the earth falling away beneath his feet.

She said, 'You know that my love goes with you.'

I drove back to Sherman Oaks on Route 5, passing minor accidents in the breakdown lane. Part of the wrench of saying goodbye, I knew, was the purely selfish feeling of bereavement, of having left a part of myself behind with her. I thought the same must be true for Laura as well. But I had only myself to blame. If I was in shock it was because I had conjured up the ghost of my youth, and seen that it was capable of bleeding.

*   *   *

I got out of the swimming-pool, on a deck built out over the side of a canyon above the fair city of Burbank, and went to answer the telephone. My friend Joe McDermott, the Orientalist, was calling from Berkeley. He hadn't yet found Rick for me, he said apologetically, because there had been a gross misunderstanding. The man he'd been thinking of turned out to be the wrong one.

It appeared that there were, in fact, two R. Wanamakers in Chinese Studies in the United States. His one was Professor Roderick Wanamaker who taught twentieth-century Chinese intellectual and political history at the University of Wisconsin, Madison. Joe had thought that Roderick might be shortened to Rick, which was why he'd searched him out. The second R. Wanamaker, my one, was quite different. His name appeared as co-author of a 1980 article, about the model commune of Da Zhai, in the American periodical *China Today*. In this, Rick was identified as being attached to the University of Michigan, Ann Arbor.

So far, so good. But Rick had since disappeared. His name was not included in the most recent *Directory for the Association of Asian Studies*. Since the *Directory* was published in Ann Arbor, and virtually all North American scholars engaged in work on China would be included in it, the likelihood was that Rick Wanamaker was not in the China field any more.

'So we're back at square one?' I asked. I couldn't believe my ill luck.

'Not yet. I'm going back to that article. If I can find out who else was involved in the Da Zhai project, I might have something for you.'

I could tell that Joe's professional pride had been caught on the raw. He wasn't going to let Rick get away from him. I wished him good luck and put the phone down. As I did so, something beside it caught my eye – a piece of paper on which were scrawled the words *Andrea Rush called you. Please ring her back.*

I grabbed the paper in case it flew away and dialled her number. Andrea came on the line. She hadn't been avoiding me. She'd got my messages and she'd been trying to make contact. She'd love to meet and talk. How about tomorrow for coffee in Berkeley, round about eleven in the Ariel Café?

First I had an appointment with Rose in her downtown office. *Rose Seeger, you remember her?* Howard had quickly turned the page of the photograph album as though he didn't want an answer. Or else his question was rhetorical, since Rose was not a woman you'd forget.

Tall, blonde, remarkably mature for her twenty years, she used to make C. think of Lana Turner. Her sensuousness was straight out of the golden age of the movies; she was bright and determined too. She played up to her Lana Turner image, but why not? Lowrie was still living in Topside, and Lowrie had the women of the house on her side. So for the time being Rose stayed aloof, sunning herself under the lemon tree and walking in the garden naked under gowns which flowed with every curve of her buxom figure. Probably she constituted an example to Andrea and the others of everything that feminism was distancing itself from. But she got her way.

She saw C. as an ally since he was an outsider like herself. One night, she and Howard invited him over to supper in the cottage (as Rose called the annexe). Howard was late. Rose started grilling the steaks in the tiny kitchen while C. sat at the table and drank Zinfandel. It was a warm, close evening; Rose was wearing a net dress over nothing at all. They listened for the growl of Howard's motorbike coming down the drive, and talked about love.

She respected C.'s relationship with Laura. It was *deep*. She wanted a relationship which was deep. Howard himself was deep; in fact he was one of the deepest people she knew, such a brainy guy, so strong-minded. Passionate too. But he kept part of himself back. He had his science lab at UCSC, and his garage/workshop out front; she had the kitchen and the bedroom, 'and, I mean, you just can't spend half of your life on a king-size waterbed'.

She sighed. The steaks sizzled.

'I don't know,' C. said innocently. 'It's a long time since I've been on a king-size waterbed.'

'Really?'

That's when they heard the sound of Howard's motorbike. He banged through the workshop door into the kitchen and glanced at C. suspiciously. Plainly he had forgotten his invitation to supper. Rose went into the bedroom. When she came out, she was wearing a gown over her net dress. Outside, crickets chirruped nervously in the stillness.

'This is a great steak,' said C.

Finding Rose thirteen years later had been easier than I'd expected. 'Somewhere in the Los Angeles area,' Howard had told me. Once, I remembered, I'd been to her mother's house in Laguna Beach, south of LA. With no other leads to go on I tried all the Seegers in the local telephone books. I struck lucky and reached her father. He had separated from Rose's Hawaiian mother years ago, but he had a couple of numbers for Rose, one of them her office at the Wilshire Medical Center in downtown Los Angeles.

Like big American hospitals tend to be, the place was clean, fresh-smelling, air-conditioned, with begonias in vases and coolly abstract prints on the walls. Glad that I was wearing an unrumpled suit, I travelled up in the elevator to the Pediatrics Department on the top floor. The receptionist was as impeccably turned out as a cosmetics saleswoman at Saks. I explained that I had an appointment with Doctor Rose Seeger. Then I sat down and waited.

After a few minutes, a door opened. A well-groomed woman in her early thirties stepped briskly towards me in a tight-fitting, slim-waisted black dress. With a careful smile she shook my hand and said,

'I've made some time. Why don't we go and talk in my office.'

Rose Seeger said that she recognized me. I couldn't return the compliment. It wasn't that physically she had changed all that much, although her hair was auburn, not blonde, and her face was broader and her mouth fuller than I recalled . . . it was because Rose had become a different woman. Lana Turner had vanished and been replaced by an exquisite amalgam of all the young women doctors in TV soaps who sashay up to the bed where the lead actor is *in extremis* and revive the first flicker of sexual interest in his vacant eyes.

Throughout the time she made for me, Rose retained the highly professional air of someone for whom the past is a folder in the filing-cabinet, to be pulled out, examined with critical detachment and replaced with a smooth click of the closing drawer. She was too young and too busy to enjoy reflecting upon the course of her life. She showed me a photograph on the window-ledge behind her desk of her good-looking husband, a lawyer, and their two attractive children aged three and five. About her family she was happy to prattle on. About Howard and the house on Spring Street she was at first reluctant to say much of anything.

I asked her what her first impressions of Topside had been.

'Well . . .'

A pause.

'I mean, you came to it via Howard, didn't you?'

'Mm. Mmhm.'

Another pause.

'How did you first meet him?'

'Howard?'

'Yes.'

'He ran a laboratory where I was studying up at the University.'

Rose had majored in psychobiology. Chemistry and Howard had been part of the curriculum. Rose had found UCSC a little flaky, like most of what was going on at that time. She didn't feel like an alumnus, any more than she'd felt a sense of belonging to Spring Street, especially when she first arrived.

'I was so consumed with the difficulties of the relationship with Howard – was it going to be established or was it not? The other thing also was that I was in the cottage, I wasn't in the main house. There was a whole *esprit de corps* over in the main house which in some ways I was envious of.'

I reminded her of Lowrie Fredericks, who had removed from the cottage and left Rose in command of the field. Rose was nodding, her face softening as she thought back.

'I was just consumed by the turmoil, it was sort of *crazy*, Spring Street. There was Howard's daughter and everything . . . I just sort of waltzed into it, but I think immediately my life changed, from happy-go-lucky college student to this . . . very *intense* relationship, and being a mother-figure. Let me just get this.'

The buzzer was sounding. Briskly she picked up the phone.

'Hallo? . . . What patient? . . . I'm going to be about half an hour. Okay, thanks.'

Rose had broken up with the first great love of her life before coming out to California. At Santa Cruz she had spent six months living by herself before moving in with Howard for her last year and a half of UCSC, and overnight becoming the mainstay of someone else's family. She was only twenty years old. I began to see what self-possession must have gone into coping with all this and the jealousies of Topside too. Hardest of all was getting a relationship with Katie.

'I could only feel for her in her struggle. She did not have a good childhood, Katie, and I could identify with that. I mean, Katie and I were in some ways so close, in age, she was so precocious and bright. But she still needed her Dad so bad, and needed a Mom . . . needed something I couldn't give her. You know: first her own Mom left her, then Lowrie left her – why should she bother with me? She saw no reason to. She saw the writing on the wall, with her Father. So we kind of co-existed and accepted each other, that's about the best it ever got.'

Somebody else who could identify with Katie's difficult childhood! It occurred to me that if Spring Street was a microcosm of the United States, half the population would be growing up scarred by childhood unhappiness. I asked Rose about Hélène, into whose room downstairs Katie had moved after Hélène left. Rose barely remembered her. Nobody had, so far. But Rick was a different matter. When I brought Rick Wanamaker's name up in Rose's office there was a long pause, then a wary, amused *Mmhm!*

She saw Rick as somebody who in his mind very much wanted to be part of the group in Spring Street, but didn't know how to be, and instead isolated himself from other people. He'd come into the kitchen after the others and take his meals by himself. It wasn't until near the end of Rose's time at the house, one day when they were high on something and ended up having a long conversation, that she was able to open up to Rick and get the same kind of response from him.

'You see, he really liked interacting, and relationships

were important to him. But in a way, you know, he was such a dark horse. I've been curious about him, to see where he would end up. I saw somebody once on the street, years later. I was in San Francisco. I could have sworn it was Rick and I went up to him.' She smiled. 'Of course, it wasn't. But I still think about him a little bit.'

It occurred to me that Howard's rather tense relationship with Rick might have had quite a lot to do with sexual jealousy. Had Howard been as possessive of her as I seemed to remember?

'Possessive!' Rose burst out laughing – this was better. 'Extraordinarily! Yeah! I mean, of girlfriends even! He . . . it's funny, I haven't thought about this in so long, but I mean he exerted enormous control over my life. A strong person is a wonderful thing,' she laughed again. 'But if you didn't agree with Howard there was no negotiating!'

I said that I hadn't talked much about her with Howard in Oakland because his wife Tessa was there. She interrupted –

'He got *married*?'

It turned out that the last time Rose had spoken to Howard was ten years ago, on the telephone, one week before her own marriage. After she had quitted Santa Cruz they both ended up East, with Howard at Stonybrook and Rose doing her Masters in Genetic Counselling. The trip to the Virgin Islands – that was the snapshot Howard had showed me – was evidently an attempt to patch up something that had already come apart at the seams. They went down to St John and stayed at the camp-ground. It was one of the last things they did together.

In this office on the top floor at the Wilshire Medical Center it seemed frivolous, even sexist, to ask Dr Rose

Seeger about our supper in the cottage and Howard's king-size waterbed. Whenever I tacked towards personal things she steered the conversation back to the present day. It was firmer ground; there was less likelihood of a younger Rose Seeger tapping her on the shoulder and saying – Hey, remember me?

'What I do here right now is run the pre-natal diagnosis side. I have four genetic counsellors and we primarily see patients who are pregnant, or who have lost their baby with congenital abnormalities and want to know what can be done to rule out similar birth defects in the future. I met my husband Tom while I was working at Harvard for a year or two on public health genetics. He was in law school; now he's a partner in a firm in Beverley Hills.'

The framed photograph on the window-sill was of a handsome older man, an Alan Alda type, posing with their two small children. Rose brought it over fondly.

'This is Tom with William and Ruth.'

They were good-looking, all-American kids with nothing of the Hawaiian chunkiness about their features of which Rose still carried a definite trace. Genetics, she would probably say, obeyed the laws of entropy like everything else. Thinking back to the beautiful half-Polynesian creature who had arrived at Topside that summer, I wondered if Rose felt as if she'd changed.

'I don't know what you remember about me,' I said carefully. 'But I remember that you were very sort of, well, *laid-back* in Spring Street. As if life was for living; tomorrow would look after itself.'

'Mmhm.'

I caught a flicker of irritation in her eyes. Hadn't she just been telling me about being burdened with the responsibilities she took on with Howard? 'I guess when I would go down to the Pacific Gardens Mall or to the beaches at that time it was easy to get into that feeling of . . . of . . .'

But whatever feeling Rose was seeking to recover it was apparently no longer within reach, because she shook her head almost indignantly and said,

'That's interesting, that you thought I was laid-back. I don't think I'm really a very *laid-back* person!'

She thought some more, tapping her pencil sharply on the table.

'I was young! I turned twenty-one there and it was . . . I mean I did that stuff! I did that relationship stuff early, and then I got married! I have absolutely the best marriage I have ever heard of. Part of it's just luck: but part is that I'd had two very intense relationships prior to that – one being Howard – and that helped me to identify the kind of characteristics I worked well with in another person. So I'm very thankful for it.'

Rose had learned the knack of turning everything that had happened to advantage. I admired her for it. Howard had been a dictator in their relationship – her phrase. *Because he was so domineering, I don't think I experienced a lot of things that other people do.* Spring Street had taught Rose a great deal about herself; she had put the experience to good use. I asked her what was her best memory of that time. The question prompted a longer pause than usual, and even more sentences abandoned and started over in the search for an admissible truth.

'What I used to love was leaving and going down to the Cooper House on Pacific Gardens Mall on a Sunday afternoon and listening to jazz. Remember that funny little band they used to have? I've gone back, and they were still there. I enjoy that attitude still, but it just is not compatible with my life at all! I'm very consumed with the present right now. I have a really good life, a little too busy – both of us are too busy – and one of the things I try to work on is to *get rid* of some of that stuff so that we can appreciate what we have.'

She stood up. I stood up. We shook hands. Rose led the way out into the bright hospital waiting-area, past mothers waiting expectantly. At Reception we shook hands once more; we exchanged pleasantries about meeting up again one day; and Rose went back to her next patient. She had been kind enough to dust down guarded memories for me on which the ink was already fading. Now the file was closed. As I went down in the elevator I imagined the shredder going to work, purposefully, efficiently, methodically, *getting rid* of that stuff. Why keep it? The present was good. The future was bright. The past was another country.

*   *   *

Driving back that afternoon to San Francisco, the rear-window stickers in front were beginning to set up a conversation. Don't Shoot, I'll Move Over said one. The next, Go On Hit Me, I Need The Money. Laura had barely encountered Rose Seeger at Topside. It seemed to me that they epitomized two different impulses in the American character: one towards the wilderness, the other towards the town. Laura was a Green Child, exhilarated by the feeling of being lonely in the universe, riven with existential fears and longings. Perhaps it was in the blood she inherited from her half-Red Indian grandfather that made her subversively unmaterialistic by the standards of most

Americans. She would have both respected and wondered at someone like Rose, who mainlined the American Dream of success and fair children and money in the bank.

I was like Laura, but living here had taught me how much tougher it was for an American to set herself outside the mainstream. In Western Europe, with its compact little societies, these impulses have existed happily side by side since the days when the Roman poet Horace wrote satires about the town mouse and the country mouse. In Britain nonconformism is an accepted way of life. A small island race with deeply ingrained laws and traditions can afford to give latitude to any number of mavericks and recusants, misfits and eccentrics. Idiosyncrasy is built into the system.

The continental United States is too vast and diverse a nation to be able to do the same. Its toleration is renowned: but paradoxically the pressure towards conformity is unrelenting. People who hail the USA as the great melting-pot tend to forget that the function of a melting-pot is to melt down. The result is like a fired alloy – strong but also brittle. Recognizing this, the vast majority of Americans identify conformity with respectability. Dissidents and free-thinkers are driven outside the system to take refuge in universities, religious communes and survivalist encampments.

Laura was earning scarcely more now, as an untenured teacher at UCLA, than she had been as a teaching assistant at UCSC in the late 1970s. She wouldn't be all that much better off when she had been awarded her doctorate and was embarked on her academic career. In comparison Rose, who had conformed, was very well rewarded.

*

I had a late breakfast in Palo Alto and was on the road soon after nine, heading up to Berkeley. Andrea had almost taken on legendary dimensions for me by now. It wasn't so much her elusiveness; it was the way the others had talked about her – Howard and Lowrie and Katie – as if she had something about her that was special. She was more vivid to Lowrie than anybody – so *theatrical*. Katie had been drawn to Andrea with her African carvings and patterns, and was paying her some kind of unconscious homage in her own silk designs. For Howard, Andrea had been the only one of his tenants who really matched up to those spectacular rooms. Whatever his private feelings about her, he hadn't grudged his respect.

Because she really wasn't like the rest of Topside. When they slumped, Andrea sparkled. Her energy and drive were infectious; she would talk and argue into the small hours, and then be up early, fresh and clear-eyed, to teach her classes at UCSC, where she was the youngest assistant professor on campus. Hearing her voice on the phone, husky and rapid like Ornette Coleman at 45 rpm, I had started thinking about the extraordinary magnetism she possessed, which attracted women and men in equal numbers. Jan and Hélène had fallen completely under her spell. The weekend after Andrea cropped her hair, both girls went into town and came back with mannish, pageboy hair-cuts which they wore proudly for the rest of the summer as a mark of their freedom from outworn symbols of femininity.

Andrea was not antagonistic to men. It was her belief, simply, that women deserved equality with them. In Chicago in the late 1960s she had been in on the very start of the women's movement, in breakaway workshops at conventions of Students for a Democratic Society, the most influential of all the student organizations which opposed the war in Vietnam. Using the tactics they'd learned in SDS, women like Andrea carried the feminist message afield. Andrea wanted women's studies incorporated into the academic curriculum at UCSC. She developed a syllabus of texts which she used as the basis of discussion by her women's groups.

In this, at any rate in Santa Cruz, she was a pioneer. But she was a leader of individuals and small groups, not of any established movement; she was too impatient and questioning for that. Her natural instinct was to challenge orthodoxies wherever she saw them. When radical feminism became an orthodoxy, in the late seventies and early eighties, I felt sure Andrea would have detached herself and moved on to something else.

But what? It was anybody's guess. Andrea never stayed in one place long enough for her friends to be objective about her. She was just back from Africa, or just off somewhere for a dialogue; and when she did stop and sit down at her round table with the candles on it, while the sun sank across her great picture window into Monterey Bay, it was never to talk about herself (as if she could have had time for herself!) but to discuss what Presidential candidate Jimmy Carter had promised to do for women, or how there had been a thirty per cent increase in the past year in student job applications to the CIA, or whether C.'s ideas of what Paradise might be had any relevance to the hopes and aspirations of the dispossessed.

Perhaps I was chary of asking too many questions. She would have laughed them off in her deprecating way and changed the subject. She may have had many men around or just one or two, and she mothered Hélène, but she showered her most demonstrative affection on the proud, beautiful Rafiki, her Abyssinian cat. All I could remember her saying about herself was that she had come from Southside Chicago like me. And that like me she had no inclination to go back.

I crossed the Bay Bridge and headed up towards the Ariel Café. A lot had changed since we'd last met. I had to be prepared for change in Andrea too. She had drawn much of her vitality from the radicalism of those days, especially from the emancipation of women. After seven years of the Reagan Presidency, radicalism had shifted its meaning, it seemed to me. People now talked about radical diets instead. *Rolling Stone* magazine, once the house journal of the politically active young, now advertised exercise machines, skin-conditioning cream and army recruitment. Out of all the revolutionary movements of the late sixties and early seventies, feminism alone had won through, with the consequence that its radicalism had mostly been ingested into the mainstream.

On every other front, utopia was as far away as ever. The gurus of the early seventies were now silent or marginalized, dragging their antique counter-culture round the lecture circuit like war veterans. Jerry Rubin was a successful businessman. Some of the others who'd battled with the pigs at the 1968 Chicago Democratic Convention had gone into religion, or into gourmet barbecue cooking.

Abbie Hoffman was the exception. Star of the Chicago 7 trial, co-founder with Rubin of the Youth International Party, mastermind behind the schemes to levitate the Pentagon and to freak out the good citizens of Chicago by pouring drugs into the water-supply, he was the only one to have kept the fire in his belly. I'd like to have met the guy. But just a week earlier, in a state of chronic depression, Abbie Hoffman had killed himself, overdosing on drugs and booze. The day after it happened, a network TV crew went to Columbia University, where Hoffman had first proclaimed Revolution for the hell of it, to ask students how they felt about his death.

None of them had heard of him. That hurt.

Mid-morning, the café on Shattuck and Cedar was only quarter-full. Across by the wall, in blue jeans and a denim jacket, sat a slim woman with a shock of blonde hair. I went over and hugged her. One look had told me that Andrea had lost none of her dazzle. The megawatt light-source within her still shone out through her vividly blue eyes; her elfin face with its freckles was more attractive than ever. She crackled with life.

In between ordering coffee and having it brought to us, we had already talked back the clock to 1976. In the interven-ing years Andrea had had a child, Oliver, born in Africa, the same age as mine. She had lived with the head of the Eritrean Liberation Front in a collective in Addis Ababa, and rewritten a major work on aid and ecology in the Third World after having had the first manuscript filched from her Addis Ababa hotel room by US intelligence. She was unmistakably . . . Andrea.

My book interested her because she had it in mind to write an autobiographical novel. We talked about memory and its almost random associative powers: how easily it could ignore the realities of a past time and place, and create other realities in their stead, thus fabricating a picture which could be as persuasive and inaccurate as any historian's. Forgetting Katie and Lowrie, I was about to tell Andrea, smugly, that my own memories of Spring Street had so far stood up to the test of time: but something stopped me – and lucky it did. Because by the time Andrea had finished talking, I knew I was wrong. There had been a whole lot of things going on, that summer, which I had misinterpreted or which had completely passed me by.

She began by clearing up the mystery of the scribbled message from Terry Hoffman which had brought C. to Spring Street in the first place. Terry Hoffman was an old lover of hers. She'd been living with him in Chicago; a passionate admirer in Berkeley had sent her a plane ticket to California.

'Don't forget to go down to Santa Cruz and see the wild flowers,' Terry Hoffman had said wryly as he saw her off.

Andrea had come down, and in the middle of the wild flowers had seen a sign, 'Environmental Studies'. She'd followed it and met the project leader and got talking to him about an environmental programme he was starting up (similar to what she was running now in Berkeley, but in the early seventies far ahead of its time) and had ended up working for him at UCSC.

Talking to Andrea it seemed that pretty much everything in her life had been as serendipitous as that. Like how she discovered Spring Street. She had been living in an A-frame right up in the hills, deep in the redwood forests. Not far away lived a couple of freaked-out radicals, typical of the weird and violent people who seemed to be drawn to this part of the world. When they started showing an interest in her she began getting frightened, she wanted to be around normal people. She got into her red VW station-wagon and drove down towards Santa Cruz, looking for somewhere on the edge. She found the neighbourhood, she found the house and she knocked on the door. That same week Howard had advertised a vacancy, the one and only time he did so. He showed Andrea the house, the yard, the garden.

'I just had to live there. Period. Finished.'

She'd had the best rooms, she needed no reminding of that, or of the times we had spent sitting round the barrel-table with the kerosene lamp on it burning steadily as we talked into the early hours.

'And candles sometimes! I used to think it was like a little temple, with my Makondi art on the walls and the beaded Masai mats and lots of music and musical instruments – Ethiopian reed-flutes, and finger-harps. And people perceived it like that. Perhaps it was the aura of the house. Everybody wanted to meet there. We had all those places at UCSC to meet, and instead everyone wanted to come to Spring Street and sit round that table, the Praxis people from HistCon, the people from Women's Studies – it was the nerve-centre of Women's Studies – and they'd play guitar and camp down in my room . . . I'll always remember Juliet Mitchell saying, *I'll never forget this place.* It was like a spiritual place. So isolated, between sky and sea; it drew everything out of people. It was the most Californian place in California!'

I summoned more coffee and nodded in an encouraging sort of way. This was what I wanted to hear. I wanted her to endorse my mental picture of how it was: a little corner of heaven where the sun shone and music played, and people from the Marxist sub-group of the History of Consciousness programme (that was Praxis) sat round a table by candle-light and prattled about the coming world revolution. Andrea was far away.

'You know, Christopher, I used to love to walk out of that house and go bird-watching, off in the meadows. Because I was trained in ecology I was very aware that as you'd go out there were four or five different vegetation community types, and I would cross-section them all and observe all the different birds and animals. In ecological terms it was an ecotone, a place in transition where different systems connected and competed with each other. It had ravines, it had live-oak, scattered savannah stuff, it had forest vestiges, it had open prairie, and it had orchards. And as it turned out, Spring Street was an ecotone in human terms as well.'

I liked this idea, of Spring Street as a place in transition where a whole range of different people connected. But not competing, surely? My recollection was that every-body in Spring Street got on pretty well together – didn't they?

Andrea looked at me wonderingly.

'I've never seen such a place of polarizations as there,' she exclaimed. Elsewhere, in other communes, there were political, ideological, cultural, sexual links. None existed at Topside, not even, so far as Andrea knew, sexual. 'Howard held down the sexual dimension of the house.'

'Did he? How?'

'In all kinds of ways. With his pawns, his little freckle-faced kids. I always thought he *chose* girls like that, and he always had them sunbathing, preferably with no clothes on. I was sickened! It was heavy, sexual, imperial; he seemed to me to be involved in a massive manipulation of these ... *children*. As a 1970s feminist I was viscerally nauseated by all this!' She laughed at her youthful indignation.

I saw now why Howard had been so reticent about Andrea; the antipathy must have worked both ways. I told her about the owners, and how Howard had come to be there, and the tears he shed over the Captain and Nannie. Andrea was astounded. It gave her an entirely new perspective on Howard; she had no idea he possessed the ability to look into himself.

'I think you must have had a closer connection to Howard than me,' she said wryly. 'I don't know. Anybody must have. I think he didn't know what to make of me and didn't really want to make anything of me, so the best thing was to disconnect. It was like a dance; a kind of managed potential conflict. It wasn't active dislike. We never clashed. It was just one of those instincts: let's not do that.'

But what about when we were all in the kitchen together or the living-room? Andrea shook her head.

'The downer in that house was Howard in the kitchen, exercising his territorial rights. My heart would *sink*. Usually he'd come in and make some cryptic remark, not necessarily hostile, such as to say – Hallo, I'm powerful and you're powerful and isn't that nice ... and you would leave. Same with the living-room. To me it was a place where you could run into Howard, so don't go there, why bother? I never was even conscious, particularly, of not liking him. We had a kind of unspoken contract, which included mutual attraction as well as mutual antipathy. He'd say to me, "Lowrie is such a child. You and I are the only adult people around here." But when Howard was doing one of his dictatorial numbers on someone in the house, especially if he didn't respect them . . .' She shrugged. 'He was very fetishistic about, say, the towels in the kitchen, or the rose-bushes, and he'd do this big number about everybody obeying the rules.'

It was true, it was coming back to me, there had been an ugly scene with Hélène, who (not for the first time) had missed her turn to take the dustbins up to the gate. C. had come in to find Hélène in tears; Howard had threatened to throw her out of the house –

'– then I would see Katie looking up at him, because she adored him so much,' Andrea went on, 'but looking up with this questioning look, like she was saying "Who are you?", "What are you?" She would see him in these horribly negative interactions with people, and I would see that question on her face and I always sympathized with that, because I grew up in parallel circumstances – maybe that's why I really tracked in to that child. It was the same with Hélène. Because I'd had a lot of pain in my childhood, I could hear her pain, which was much worse than mine. But Katie! I loved Katie. I actually worried about her there – because even in 1976 I had this fantasy of family life, the one that got me into marriage, and with the wrong man! Katie was growing up in this bizarre life. Even back then, when nobody thought of our lives as bizarre. God, I'd love to see her now.'

She talked about Rick, whom she liked okay and got along with fine. 'But Rick for me was a Jewish, Chicago, intellectual, nice, kind of tortured Jewish boy, and I felt I'd known him all my life, you know? Unlike you, in that house. You were really mysterious to me. I mean, you were smart and you were sensitive and I really liked you as a person. But I couldn't ever . . . get you nailed!'

She was laughing, teasing me. I muttered something about how much I'd changed in Spring Street, though perhaps she was back in Africa by the time it showed. But I wasn't taking in what she was saying: I was thinking about Hélène.

Hélène . . . she'd been happy enough, surely? Of course there'd been fads – but I imagined her embarking on them with the kind of eager innocent enthusiasm she showed for anything new. She'd gardened with the rest of us, and sunbathed with Lowrie and Rose, and darted around the house, gamine, unwary, almost more of a child than eleven-year-old Katie.

Andrea had no memory of Jan and Hélène cutting their hair short in imitation of her. She stared at me. 'Isn't that funny? I had no awareness of their . . .' she paused, 'of that level of attraction to me. I loved Jan: she was one of my students, and generally I saw my students as my younger siblings. Nowadays I see them as my children!' She laughed wryly. 'But Jan was also a colleague, a political *comrade* in the 1970s sense. I was very deeply connected around the farmworkers' scene; and my students were involved, and Jan was so into that. I never saw her as looking up to me particularly. If she did, I wasn't aware of it.

'Hélène was different. Jan was more like a little sister and Hélène was a child, you know. She was a confidante of mine, in the way that she might have confided in a mother, or had a mother confide in her. She was like a wounded bird I had to take under my wing; her childhood was terrible, and that's why she needed so much help. Maybe it's because I've had a couple of students commit suicide, but I've often wondered if she wasn't actually almost para-suicidal at times, or just in intense despair.'

'This is Hélène?'

I was appalled. I couldn't believe we were talking about the same person. What terrible childhood? Hélène had never let on, in all the times she had sat on the sun-terrace with C. and chatted away. What was this dreadful secret? Andrea didn't go into details. She said something about 'levels of abuse' which had destroyed Hélène's confidence and left her always seeking close relationships which never worked out.

'Really?'

A sudden picture flashed into my mind of a dapper little guy in his mid or late twenties with curly black hair and a yellow waistcoat. This was Boris, the 'boyfriend' everybody had been hearing about, the one she said was a Russian pianist. The household welcomed him, but he was oddly elusive. He came around once or twice. C. never saw him after that.

I had to find Hélène. I needed to talk to her. Andrea was doubtful. She couldn't remember her surname. Hélène – Hélène Mackintosh? something like that – she thought might be traceable through a Community Services project in the San Joaquin Valley. Hélène could be anywhere. She had continued to ring up Andrea with her problems for several years after she left Spring Street, and then the phone calls stopped coming. Perhaps she was in Europe. Perhaps she was dead. Andrea was frightened for her, frightened there could have been an implosion. Hélène had been so tight, so intense, and becoming more so. Anything could have happened to her. Anything at all.

Andrea had a class to take. I knew there was something I

had to ask her ... something she'd said. About the place she'd lived in before coming to Spring Street, the *violence*, what did she mean?

Andrea was getting up. I followed her outside.

She said, 'After what I'd gone through, Spring Street was a haven, you see.'

She hugged me, got into her car and drove away.

That was it? I stood on the sidewalk and watched her disappear into the traffic on Shattuck. In two or three days she would be in Africa. 'When I get back,' she'd said, 'we must talk again.' But where would I be by then? I'd had my picture of Spring Street nicely sketched out; Andrea had breezed in and repainted it, then breezed out again. Of course, Andrea did *dramatize* so much ... but everything she'd said about that summer, about Spring Street and the people in it, rang true.

I felt a sort of resentment, mingled with a growing anxiety. I'd come out here looking for a missing person – myself – in the complacent belief that the other people in the frame would be more or less as I remembered them. But the summer, C.'s summer, was taking on such a different perspective that I was beginning to wonder how much it said about me. The vision of Eden was darkening: shadows were advancing up the grass.

*   *   *

As Proust declared – and it could be the epigraph to his masterpiece – the true paradises are those which are lost to us. The original Christian vision of the earthly paradise faded centuries ago. It began to dim from that moment, at the beginning of the fifteenth century in Italy, when Adam and Eve unfix themselves from their painted background and for the first time appear before us as human beings born to suffer and die. Nowhere is this miracle more dramatic than in the Brancacci Chapel of the Carmelite church in Florence. High on a corner of the right-hand wall, in a fresco by the painter Masolino trained in the late-medieval International Gothic style, Adam and Eve stand in a graceful pose under the serpent-entwined Tree. In their movements are the beginnings of realism, but their gestures are formal, hieratic. Their eyes stare unseeingly into space.

On the opposite wall is the famous fresco of the Expulsion, which Masolino's young pupil and colleague Masaccio completed in about 1425. Adam and Eve are stumbling away from the gates of Eden. Adam's head is bowed; his hands are pressed to his face. Eve has her arms across her breasts, squashing them slightly. With her other hand she covers her private parts. Her head is tossed back and her mouth is open in a howl of grief and shame, shocking in its abandon. Their naked bodies have the weight and natural muscular proportions of the Florentine market folk whom Masaccio on his scaffolding would have seen below, offering up their prayers. It is as if, falling from the linearity of Masolino's *Temptation*, they have taken on the true proportions of the human race along with its understanding of the difference between good and evil.

The development of perspective in Florentine art went side by side with the development of a perspective upon history. In the world they inhabited, as in the pictures they drew, the pioneers of the Renaissance began to visualize themselves in the foreground, giving depth and focus to the world around them. They were constantly experimenting, testing their knowledge and their judgement against the observable world, in the confident belief that everything in God's creation had an organic cause and a purpose which they could turn to their advantage. The perfect proportions of Classical sculpture and architecture, which the Gothic age still looked upon as sacrilegious, were studied by men like Brunelleschi and Donatello not so that they could be superstitiously imitated but in a spirit of scientific inquiry.

To artists of the Renaissance, the Genesis story provided an entirely permissible means to demonstrate the beauty and nobility of the naked human form. They naturally ascribed their scientific approach to divine illumination. Antique statuary could be used as a model because it was the oldest extant art, and its figures were therefore the closest to God's creation. But the consequence was that the perception of Adam and Eve in fifteenth and sixteenth century Europe shifted away from their dreadful sin. They continued to speak to the faithful about disobedience and death, but they did so in the proud knowledge that they were the first parents of a superior race. And for the first time the Church began to have difficulty controlling and checking the pursuit of knowledge for its own sake.

In the Middle Ages the Classical world had usually been summoned up (except by a few farsighted men like Petrarch and Boccaccio) to demonstrate its feebleness in contrast with the Christian era. It was a commonplace of scholastic rhetoric, for instance, to compare the nostalgic fiction of the Golden Age with the stern facts of the biblical story. For the circle of brilliant and creative men with whom Lorenzo de' Medici surrounded himself in Florence in the 1470s, the fiction and fact were both manifestations of a higher truth about man's dream of Paradise – of a time without suffering, guilt or sin in which love ruled every heart.

It was Lorenzo de' Medici who exalted the Golden Age into a political credo for the Florentine Renaissance. At a tournament in Florence in 1469 he wore a silk scarf embroidered with roses, some fading, some fresh, and inscribed in pearls *Le temps revient*. The phrase was adapted from Virgil's fourth *Eclogue*, in which Virgil foretells the birth of a marvellous child who will bring back the golden time of peace and love as it was in the first age of man.

This earthly paradise without the snake in the grass is not Eden at all, but Arcadia. To look at Titian's *Fête Champêtre*, painted not long after 1500, is to see how rapidly the pastoral mode took over the setting of the earthly paradise. There is no hint of sacrilege in Titian's picture. The nude women, painted with a classical simplicity, expound the Renaissance belief that the beauty of the human body expresses the beauty of God's universe. It is Arcadia, but it is also the countryside outside Venice with a farm in the background and a shepherd looking on with his flock. Whether the two young Venetian gentlemen are visiting Arcadia, or whether, as they sit and play music on the sunny hillside, Arcadia has quietly enveloped them, in a vision of beauty and sweet melody – who knows?

Some of the greatest triumphs of human beauty are in the frescoes of the Temptation by Michelangelo and Raphael in the Vatican. The naked forms of Adam and Eve glory in their strength and shapeliness. Their gestures are proudly assured; they are exalted by their own magnificence. This high point of Renaissance art marks a watershed for the Christian version of the myth of Eden. The more consistently it emerged in the art and literature of the next three hundred years that Man was his own ideal, first in his physical shape and then in his moral state at the beginning, the more the Genesis narrative lost its force as a Christian parable and took on other meanings or none at all.

Milton's *Paradise Lost* ends with Adam and Eve walking hand in hand out of the Garden of Eden with everything to aim for, having attained a self-knowledge and a moral knowledge which seem to increase their stature, not diminish it. And so it will always seem, from this time onwards. For what sounds in *Paradise Lost*, in the pride of Satan and the determined curiosity of Adam, is the voice of the individual. Not the individual as Renaissance prince, be it said, but the plain man in a society of plain men each with a firm belief in the freedom of thought to range to the limit of its capacity, and the opportunity to gain, in this world, *A Paradise within thee, happier far*.

At the cost of this extraordinary development – the love of man defying the love of God – Milton kept alive the idea of paradise as the promise and goal of salvation. Within twenty years, the English philosopher John Locke was employing the Genesis story in the second of his two *Treatises of Government* as a working model of a primitive society which had no need of rulers to ratify it. Jean-Jacques Rousseau develops the theme in the first secular version of the myth of Eden to carry conviction. In his *Discourse on Inequality* he argues that Man in a state of nature needed no blessing from heaven to make him happy. His ignorance was bliss. He was immortal, back then, not because he survived for ever but because he had no conception of death. He lived from day to day, in wholeness, like the noble savage who *lives within himself, while the social man lives constantly outside himself, and only knows how to live in the opinion of others*.

It remained for the philosopher Kant, towards the end of

the eighteenth century, to improve on Rousseau by arguing that it was precisely the vicious, anti-social side of man's nature which puts him in the way of self-improvement, and that without that first attempt at free choice there would have been no chance of eventual perfection. Over a space of three hundred years the Christian myth of Eden had been stood on its head. Adam and Eve have become the first romantic heroes, suffering and dying for the sake of the destiny of the human race.

*   *   *

From the Ariel Café I drove a few blocks west to see Joe McDermott, in the Berkeley house he was renting from an Orientalist on sabbatical. He greeted me solemnly and led me inside, and poured out two glasses of a very good Californian wine. I looked at him. Joe didn't drink much, let alone at this time in the morning.

'We're celebrating,' he said. 'You can raise your glass to the best detective in the business.'

'Oh yes?'

'I've located Rick Wanamaker for you. He's living in Detroit.'

Joe had done a great job. He'd checked back on the Da Zhai project and discovered who'd been in charge of it – someone at the Far Eastern Center in Chicago. He remembered Rick well; had been sorry to lose him. But Rick had given up Chinese studies. In fact he had given up the academic life altogether. He'd taken up the law, and could be found on the end of a telephone in the carpeted offices of Perelman, Johnson and Weissmuller on the twenty-fifth floor of the 1st National Building in central Detroit.

I thought back to Rick in his Mao jacket hoeing the vegetable garden, Rick singing the praises of the Chinese Revolution to his students from a prone position on the living-room floor. I wondered aloud what had brought about this transformation.

'Well, that's interesting,' said Joe. I could almost see the twinkle in his eye, the head cocked a little to one side. 'When you see him, ask him about the Da Zhai project.'

'Why?'

'Ask him why it went wrong.'

To get into a plane in California and get out in Detroit is a weird transition. You can't help but feel that you've made a mistake. I have known people who, thirty years on, still had a chip on their shoulder about being in the wrong fraternity house in college. Detroit was like that; it was full of blameless, likeable people who thought they ought to be somewhere else. Anywhere else. Despite lavish efforts by the municipality and private enterprise, one-third of Detroit's population had already left Downtown for the suburbs.

I caught an airport bus to a Downtown hotel and checked in my bags. It wasn't yet evening but the man in front of me still looked over his shoulder as he walked down the block and hurried up some steps. They led to the overhead monorail, the PeopleMover, which linked the Renaissance Center with other secure environments where people with wallets in their pockets worked and shopped in the comforting presence of security guards. Down in the dingy streets below, people without wallets in their pockets drank and fought and took drugs and mugged each other for loose change. Or so the people up above believed. What was Rick doing here?

I thought what Howard had said about him. The little blue Mao cap with the red star. The Jewishness – *'Some mother's son, you know, who really expected more than the world owed him; and here was I, this gentile, brought up to live in the woods by himself and go miles and never come home. And I guess we were these two young men who really didn't understand what they'd inherited, really, or what culture was on their shoulders, thousands of years each . . .'*

All of them had been struck by Rick. Most of them recalled him vividly: with amusement, with impatience, with affection. Katie had spoken of his girlfriends. Rose Seeger had gone up and introduced herself on the street, years later, to somebody who resembled Rick – very unlike Dr Seeger. And now here he was, in the plushly anonymous reception area of Perelman, Johnson and Weissmuller, smiling uncertainly and putting out his hand.

I saw at once about the girlfriends. Rick was strikingly good-looking, more so than I remembered, with bushy black hair, melancholy brown eyes and a strong face softened by a wide, rather feminine mouth. He wore a suit and tie as if he still wasn't used to them.

'I'm one floor down,' he said. 'Let's go this way. We aren't supposed to show clients the back stairs, but waiting for the elevator can take ten minutes.'

He showed me into his office on the twenty-fourth floor, with an awesome view over the city.

'I knew who you were right away,' he said, 'though I didn't remember your face when we talked on the phone. How did you find me?'

I told him ('The other R. Wanamaker is a Catholic,' he interrupted drily) and then started bringing my facts up to date. During the summer of 1976 Rick had been on the UCSC faculty on temporary assignment, teaching Chinese politics as a replacement for someone who was abroad. After three years he'd had to look for another post. He ended up in a non-tenured job at Michigan State University. This was 1978. A week after he got there, 'probably due to the solid family values of the Midwest', he met his wife-to-be. Moira had one child from a previous marriage. Within eighteen months there was another baby, and suddenly Rick was a family man.

'Is that why you gave up Chinese studies?'

Rick shrugged. He lifted his hands from the desk. The prospect of academic insecurity . . . wandering around the country taking one-year jobs, no tenure . . . basically it was an economic decision. He was heading towards forty, and his last pay at Michigan State, in 1981, was $18,000 a year.

He spoke defensively. He'd been part of what another academic I'd been to see had called 'the revolution of lowered expectations' to describe the career curve of himself and other 1970s Santa Cruz graduate students who'd gone on to teach. Even so, I felt sure that this couldn't be the whole story.

'Most of my best students had lost any interest in academic work,' Rick explained. 'They weren't interested in the Chinese revolution. They were all rushing off to law school or to business school for a Masters degree, or becoming investment bankers or business lawyers.' He'd see young students crossing the campus with books on Risk Management under their arms.

This wasn't like Santa Cruz. This was the 1980s at

Michigan State. 'My job, from the undergraduates' point of view, was to facilitate their rise up the ladder,' Rick said wryly. All his students cared about was getting grades that would look good on their CVs. They had no time for ambiguity or subtlety, no time for doubt. Told what to think, they scribbled industriously. Asked what they thought, they looked at their watches. When Rick asked them difficult questions they sulked, as though he was doing them out of their future. Study had to be cost-effective. If you believed in absorbing knowledge for its own sake, you got left behind.

I knew what he was saying. It was a theme of all the teachers I spoke to in the United States, and not only there. A university contemporary of mine was personnel director of a London merchant bank. Awestruck, he described to me the twenty-one-year-old high-fliers who came to him for a job in the City. Their first-class degrees were just the beginning. They had a Blue or a half-Blue in some Oxbridge sport to give them leverage with clients who respected that sort of thing; they were well advanced in studying Japanese so that they could offer to help with the Tokyo market; and in their vacations they had done charity work, since that too went down well with interviewing boards. These people were as alien to him, and me, as our 1960s generation must have been to our own parents. 'Where did their childhood go?' he wanted to know. 'What's going to stop them cracking up in later life?'

Rick was my generation. His college days had coincided with the civil rights movement, to some extent the anti-Vietnam War movement also. He had gone into Chinese studies because Chinese communism was the greatest revolutionary experience of the twentieth century and he was fascinated by the political lessons to be drawn from it. The students he confronted in seminars at Michigan State University in the early 1980s could not have been more different from him. They must have seemed eerily like communist cadres, except that theirs were the doctrines of capitalism. Impatient with argument, they wanted to be told what was right.

'Finally I said to myself – Why am I banging my head against the wall? I could be a better lawyer than these people. I might as well do it.'

So Rick went to law school, alongside some of his pupils. He married Moira. He joined the firm of Perelman, Johnson and Weissmuller, with its congenial atmosphere and excellent pay prospects.

'Basically I spend most of my time working on big real-estate deals. Fifteen years ago I would have laughed at myself for what I'm doing now. I would have thought it wasn't personally or politically appropriate.' But he enjoyed his work; he was happy enough. Except that he really wanted to move . . . to California.

'Back to the West Coast!' I stared at him. Rick was serious. 'But everybody thought . . . I mean, you seemed a bit out of place at Spring Street. My perception of you in 1976 was as someone who wasn't enjoying California at all and wanted to move back East!'

Rick considered this at length.

'I think I'm a mixed personality,' he said. 'I have a tendency to be a little unhappy wherever I am. That period in California – there were a lot of things going on that meant I wasn't necessarily a happy person from time to time.'

Relationships, for one thing. An Easterner, he missed the

Eastern intensity. Resentful that he didn't have a regular job at UCSC, he was envious of people who did.

'I was having trouble getting my career off the ground, and I used to think that people who lived in Santa Cruz had a wonderful life ... some of the very basic things like weather and climate and scenery and ocean and sunlight, and people's way of relating to it all.'

And the students at UCSC. Rick had praise for them. Compared with the undergraduates at Michigan State they were easier-going, more mature, better-rounded human beings. At the time he was critical of them for not working hard enough and for thinking it reasonable that a certain part of every day should be set aside for pleasure. The anti-puritan ethic was alive and well in Santa Cruz in the late 1970s. Rick didn't realize how much it had got to him until he went back East in 1979. The people around him seemed to be different. They were unphysical; you couldn't touch anybody in a casual way. People in elevators moved to the four corners. Nobody talked to each other in passing, say in a store or a bank, whereas in Santa Cruz it had been natural to talk idly to strangers.

'So why don't you just move back?'

He shrugged again. Job mobility wasn't a problem, although the house prices in LA right now were daunting. But there were the children.

'California's a wonderful place for an adult to move to and relax, but maybe not the healthiest place for your kids to grow up.'

Rick had found the same problem everybody found who moved to California from the older world. It was hard to shift beyond the superficial level of relationships. You could be good friends for years with people whose last names you didn't know, or what they did for a living. People connected and moved on like cells in the bloodstream. Sexual intimacy was easy; spiritual intimacy was much harder to find. Rick in Santa Cruz spent most of his life chasing women around. When he moved back East he was amazed how quickly he settled down. California was an ideal place to go, he'd worked out, if you've grown up in the East or Midwest where your character and moral bearings have had a chance to mature. But he'd been no more than a post-adolescent, during the time in Spring Street.

'Most academics really spend the years between twenty and thirty-five having their adolescent problems. Which in some ways is good too, because it keeps a lot of their aliveness. But I think Howard and I really hit head-on like that . . .'

It was Andrea (it was always Andrea) who had got him into Topside. They had known each other vaguely in Chicago, where they had both belonged to the graduate membership of Students for a Democratic Society. Rick had recently arrived in Santa Cruz and was having tremendous problems finding a place to live. The only available accommodation by that time was in unpleasant, expensive apartments on the fringes of town. Andrea told him someone was moving out of Spring Street; he had to go and be interviewed by Howard Tellier. The rent was just $165 a month.

'I passed the interview, although,' a slow smile, 'I think he later regretted it.'

This antagonism, which had pretty much passed me by, was as vividly remembered by Rick as by Howard, although with greater self-deprecation. Howard was difficult, but he'd been difficult too. Things had come to a head when he'd moved out of the big front room he used to have into Andrea's room, after Andrea moved up to Berkeley.

'I figured I was living in heaven when I moved in there – that big sleeping-porch where you could look out and see the ocean, and the sun . . . I still miss the sun on that house, I have the most sensual images of the sunlight.'

Howard kept on threatening to evict Rick from heaven and move in himself. One time he started a tirade while Rick was tripping, out on the patio with his French girlfriend.

'I don't know whether you've been on acid or not, but it's the kind of thing where your mind is so far away and in a different sphere that it's very hard to deal with normal conversations. Francine and I were sitting quietly and communicating within the drug, and Howard suddenly came out and said, "Rick, I've got to talk to you! I've been thinking of taking your room again!" It was just devastating. Like being hit over the head with a sledgehammer.'

Before Howard left, to go and spend a year at Stonybrook, things mellowed between them. Howard gave Rick an enormous cast-iron frying-pan, which he still uses. The others in Spring Street had a more sketchy existence in his memory. Lowrie Fredericks he only remembered as a kind of foster-mother to Katie. Rose Seeger, and her sisters who both came to live at Spring Street after C. had gone, he remembered with real affection.

'Those three were real Los Angelenos. One was prettier than the next, I tell you, very free and easy and beautiful. One thing I'll say for Howard, he always managed to choose attractive women for that place.'

Me he claimed to remember vividly. He associated me, for some reason, with Hélène. I reminded him of Laura, the sleeping-bag, the black eye received from her boyfriend. Rick skirted round these matters with a lawyer's tact. He hadn't got on with Hélène, although it might have been his fault as much as hers.

'She was real nice-looking. But I always felt that she had a lot of problems.' Jan, too – 'A very curious person. I tried to be great friends with her, but it didn't work out.' He didn't think she was very happy living in Spring Street, except maybe when she was helping him dig the vegetable garden which he started – 'She was kind of a farm type.'

He lapsed into silence. My arrival had filled him with restlessness. I could see that, after five years, he still couldn't quite believe that he was here, sitting at a desk, conveyancing clients' real estate. As we got up to meet his wife for dinner at the Rattlesnake Club he picked up a package and for a moment didn't recognize the name of the law firm on the next floor down.

'You know, I was there for three years,' he said. 'Longer than anybody. And I thought, as I was leaving for another lousy teaching job, that I will never ever again live in a house as splendid as this one. Probably that was true.'

Rick's wife Moira had dressed up smart and come in from the northern suburbs for dinner with us in the Rattlesnake Club. She was blonde and pretty, buxom, with an uncompromising practicality which complemented Rick's air of benign dreaminess. She eyed her husband warily as he talked nostalgically about Spring Street . . . how it had got wilder after I left, with nude parties and hot-tubbing. His strait-laced Midwestern father had turned up for one of the parties, and let his hair down . . .

It seemed longer than thirteen years ago: it was a different generation, a different outlook on life entirely. The students and young lawyers they met nowadays were always in a hurry, always pressing on, uninterested in relaxation, or culture, or foreign travel except on business, because they were entirely motivated by the fear that they *weren't making enough money*, that their peers were overtaking them and would be able to afford the yacht and the country-club weekend at a younger age, while they were still working their butts off.

The younger generation – they were consumed by impatience, the young lawyers too. The law was okay but it moved too slowly to satisfy their urgency to be rich. All they talked about and thought about was saving money to invest in something that would make them a fortune. Rick listened to them discussing it. One good business deal and they would be there, just one . . .

These were the children of 1960s parents, some of them now in their first jobs, impatient, hungry for leadership, for being told what was right, because they were under too much time pressure to work things out for themselves. Moira agreed. Recently her seventeen-year-old had been at a school debate on flag-burning, after some protester had set fire to the Stars and Stripes. Not a single one of the kids had allowed it to be a permissible right. They all condemned it as a criminal act. Reagan had been a hero to them. They didn't want to know about the druggy, loose-living seventies. The drugs taken by young people in the Wanamakers' middle-class Detroit suburb weren't crack or cocaine or even marijuana; they were alcohol and chew-tobacco, as if they were in a time-warp of the 1950s.

Rick had been trying to persuade his stepson to let his

hair grow. No chance. The boy wanted it short and neatly parted like all his friends who were seventeen going on sixty. Rick laughed and looked tenderly at Moira.

'We feel younger than our children,' he said.

I went along with that. I felt the same frisson he often did when I was with people of that age, some of them in their late teens, some in their late twenties or even touching thirty, balding a little on top, frowning, serious, impatient, shooting their cuffs. It was one of the mysteries I was setting out to solve with this book – what right did people of my generation have to feel so lucky?

The fact remained: Rick had been a radical back then; now he was a real estate lawyer. I wanted to talk about Da Zhai, the Chinese village which had been the subject of his doctoral thesis. *Ask him why it went wrong*, Joe McDermott had said.

It turned out that while I had been working on ideas of Paradise, Rick had been pursuing his own utopia. Da Zhai was widely known in China as a model Maoist commune, because of its apparent ability to increase production through political study and hard work free of any modern technology. As a graduate student from the University of Chicago, Rick had travelled widely in China in 1972, just after Nixon went. At that time he was living in Berkeley doing research and taking part in SDS protests against the corruption of the market-led economy and against the war in Vietnam. Da Zhai must have appealed to him as the ideal paradigm of the revolutionary alternative – a self-sustaining community in which people were not powerless statistics, and their civil rights extended to control of what they produced.

During the middle and late seventies, Rick researched Da

Zhai, attempting a reasoned and scholarly explanation of the commune and its history. His thesis had its own integrity, as a breakwater against the tide of materialism which increasingly was sweeping his students away. It was evidence that capitalism was not the only way forward, that history was not always on the side of the rich and the powerful.

Then after Mao Tse-tung's death, as his hardline conservative supporters began to be purged from the Central Committee and a more centralized economy asserted itself, disturbing news began coming out of China. It was claimed that Da Zhai had in fact received all kinds of special aid from Chinese and foreign sources, including irrigation pumps of the kind not found in ninety-nine per cent of China's villages then. Peking further let it be known that there had been widespread corruption and abuse of power by the local brigade heads. Da Zhai had been a Potemkin village, a tool of Maoist propaganda.

Unfortunately this was exactly what a number of Rick's colleagues had been speculating all along. They had thought it naïve and overly sympathetic to China to take Da Zhai seriously. Now the project was aborted they lost no time in saying so. Rick got his doctorate, but he was never able to publish his thesis as a book.

'It was good work,' he said ruefully. 'The interpretation was brilliant. Whether the facts were right is another question. Da Zhai may have been more successful than people admit, but the Chinese leadership turned against it because they didn't like the economic theory behind it. But I'm not in a position now to know the answer.'

Failure to publish lost Rick job opportunities that would otherwise have come his way. There was no doubt in his mind about that. It was one reason for moving out of China studies. But the larger reason was now apparent to me. The revolutionary alternative had failed. The balloon of Maoism had lost its hot air. Looking around his students at Michigan State, it must have occurred to Rick that history was indeed on the side of the winners in a market economy. He knew that the way forward was to close the door on the past.

My appearance had fanned the embers of the old Rick, the one I remembered. He was anxious to bring the conversation back to Spring Street. He had some revisionist thoughts to share with me on the subject of Howard. In spite of everything, he thought, Howard at Topside had achieved what he set out to achieve. He had established the right kind of environment which was orderly and well maintained. After Howard left to go East, some really serious, old-style hippies took over running the house, led by Phil, 'a kind of straggly-type vegetarian' who worked for a gardening company, and Alice, who was an illustrator.

'Why did Howard pick them?'

'He wanted to keep out David and Judy from taking over.' (David was an est trainee, wedded to the psycho-babble of the Esalen Institute, who came to Topside after I left and used regularly to take over the living-room for seminars in how to achieve self-realization.) 'Phil was handy at carpentry, gardening, stuff like that. But he and Alice were less interested in the house as a whole. At first they were enthusiastic about keeping the grounds up, but there wasn't the same atmosphere. In many ways I preferred Howard, now I think about it. I don't remember such a pleasant time after Howard left.'

I said that Phil was still there, after ten years. It explained a lot about the dilapidated state of the place. Rick nodded.

He was pensive. Around us, waiters were clearing the tables and dusting the tablecloths with little brushes for the late sitting. He wanted to go back West. His brother was in Los Angeles, trying his hand at screenwriting – that was the place to be. If property prices weren't so high ... if the children weren't in school ... Santa Cruz didn't have the same intensity, but compare it with Detroit!

'Santa Cruz, you could be working with the sun streaming in, you could go to the beach at lunch-time – and I used to think of the people back in Chicago who would save their money for a couple of years just so they could take a leak out there. Which is the life I lead now. I live here in the cold. I work fifty weeks a year, and I go for a week to some warm place and wish I lived there . . .'

Moira was looking anxious. Rick gazed at her. He leaned across the table and took her hand and squeezed it.

'Let's go back?' he said.

*   *   *

There is a track I have never managed to hunt down of the great violinist Jascha Heifetz playing one of Gershwin's songs from *Porgy and Bess*. It's not in any of the London catalogues; maybe I'm hearing things but I don't think so, because I can recall now every note of that solo violin, not romantically fierce and passionate as it is in his Beethoven Violin Concerto but sliding and stretching Gershwin's tune in a deliberately playful glissando, as if not to let us forget that the maestro is *condescending*. During that summer Andrea was seeing a lot of Bob Heifetz, a tall, restless, faintly disconsolate presence in the house, so that could be why his father's violin swoops like wind shear through those sunlit rooms –

Christopher Hudson

The words that you're li'ble
To read in the Bible –
They ain't necessarily so . . .

Nothing was necessarily so any longer. As the spring of
1976 turned into summer, C. felt as though he had begun to
slip off the edge of the known world into a *terra incognita*
which observed different rules. The sun still rose and set,
bleaching the blue Pacific as it sank into the evening sea.
Days passed. People got up, played games, lay in the sun,
attended classes, made love, took out books from the library
and turned their pages. But C.'s sense of a continuum was
disappearing. Everything was here, and now. Even the
Bicentennial celebrations, in which all of Santa Cruz
participated, wasn't to widen his perspective.

Leaning on the crush barriers near the ID Building and
eating a jamoca almond fudge icecream C. watched the
Fourth of July Independence Day parade go by, along Cedar
Street, Mission Street and the Pacific Gardens Mall. After
the bell-ringing and the Victorian fire-hose cart-race, he
observed Don Gaspar de Portola on horseback, accompanied by his band of soldiers, priests and Indians,
rediscover the San Lorenzo River, which he first set eyes on
in 1769. After Don Gaspar came the floats, and after the
floats a parade of vans and mobile homes their sides open
to reveal tepee interiors with the local citizenry gussied up
as Red Indians with tomahawks and wampum-belts, their
squaws posing in fetching bits of deerskin and leather.

It made C. realize, as never before, how distant he was
from the Old World. This part of California hadn't even
been explored, let alone colonized, by Europeans before the
American Revolution. Other than a handful of Spanish

missionaries, the first Europeans to settle in Santa Cruz didn't arrive for another sixty-five years after the Liberty Bell in Philadelphia had rung out Independence in 1776. The myth which reverberates through centuries of American history, that America is a second Eden in which man started afresh with a new line of credit from God, is all the more potent on the West Coast because of its detachment from the European civilization which discovered the New Golden Land. The only real linkage even to the *American* past was a frail paper-chain of exhortations ... the Declaration of Independence, the Constitution, the Gettysburg Address.

What C. was watching was a re-creation of myth, not of history. Britain, in which probably a majority of Santa Cruzians shared some common ancestry, was represented in the national Bicentennial celebrations by equivalent tokens of a semi-mythical heritage – the Queen herself on a State Visit, the Royal Shakespeare Company, the King's College Choir and the Royal Ballet. History – real history – happened a long way away. Somewhere – Washington? Geneva? – the Americans and the Russians were signing a treaty limiting the force of underground nuclear explosions. In Britain, the Liberal Party leader Jeremy Thorpe resigned his office, facing allegations of homosexuality.

In the past – the *past* – I would have followed the progress of these events; I would have discussed them and argued over them as if they mattered to me; I would have probably written about them for a newspaper. But in reality how marginal they were, how trivial in the great scheme of things! What a fool I'd been to suppose that life was about boxy offices and rain-swept streets and the nine o'clock news, when out there the turning world offered such variety of sensual pleasures – of birdsong, sunlight, roses, Mondavi wine, and Laura whose love was a distillation of all these things.

The closest C. came to current events was flicking idly through the latest titles in the Santa Cruz bookshops. The fiction bestsellers that summer – Irving Wallace, Robert Ludlum, Ira Levin, Helen MacInnes – explored well-worn themes of Cold War good-and-evil. The non-fiction tables were freighted with guilt trips about McCarthy (Lillian Helman's *Scoundrel Time*), Nixon (Woodward and Bernstein's *The Final Days*) and Vietnam (C. D. B. Bryan's *Friendly Fire*). C. meditated on St Augustine's celebrated explanation of free will – that our first parents were super-human in potential and childlike in inexperience. So it was for the American Adam in the Second Eden – supercharged with potential and inexperience, poised on the brink of dis-illusionment.

Home at Topside, C. sat outside on the stone terrace with Hélène, his feet up on the parapet. Hélène was nineteen years old and full of curiosity about Europe, which for some reason she had set her heart on visiting. Did he remember the *événements* of May 1968? Perhaps he'd been involved in them, out there on the barricades?

She listened wide-eyed as C. reminisced nostalgically about the first anti-Vietnam demonstration outside the American Embassy that year . . . not just the banners and the shouted slogans but the feeling of solidarity with young people across the world and the extraordinary sense of power and *rightness* that buoyed them up and carried them along, past the lines of helmeted policemen, to Grosvenor Square, until only a single row of parked cars and the rumour of GIs with machine-guns behind the locked glass doors of the Embassy held them back from the target of their joyous rage . . . until the police regrouped on horseback and charged in V-formation to split the massed ranks of protest, flailing with long sticks in a panic at the vanguard, while inside the Embassy the US Ambassador lifted the telephone and delivered a mild rebuke to the Home Secretary for having allowed the mob so close to his front steps.

C. had been there, in a blue corduroy jacket, a loose silk scarf round his neck, shouting himself hoarse before going and catching the coach back to Cambridge. Joy was never again so unconfined: the police were out in force for subsequent demonstrations.

Faute de révolution, il faut faire l'amour. This was the Age of Aquarius: and if our generation couldn't transform the world (until such time as mass self-awareness brought about universal harmony) they could transform themselves. Banners and scarves were put aside and replaced with floaty kaftans and the smell of joss-sticks and patchouli oil. Forget the crisis of capitalism: brown cubes of hashish, crumbled in the fingers into cigarette-tobacco, imparted a profound significance to simpler things – to a girl telling the beads on her necklace, and to the slow dance of heated blobs of oil, forming and re-forming on the slides projected on to screens at the Arts Lab in Tottenham Court Road.

High, in his flat in Covent Garden, C. played *Blood, Sweat and Tears* and discovered the meaning of life in a *Variation on a Theme by Erik Satie.* He dilated his eyes at the candle and watched the twin flames dance together and apart in time to the music . . . he watched his hand, on the carpet beside him, move around like a snake, sinuous. This was the new transcendental reality. With God disproved – courtesy of Nietzsche, Wittgenstein, Ryle, Ayer and other fashionable philosophers – transcendence no longer had to be worked for. It was available on the tip of the tongue, on the drag of a cigarette.

C. extolled the late sixties to Hélène like a pioneer boasting of the first crossing of the Rockies to a kid who skis at Aspen. When she told him that his generation had made some incredible history, he accepted it modestly as his due. But this summer in Spring Street was turning out to be every bit as funky as his adolescence had been. In fact C. felt as if he was right back there in the sixties, except transported from his rather grimy Covent Garden flat to the very nexus of flower-power, a Gandalf's Garden of Delight.

The quality of the moment was what mattered. Synchronicity. C. found Jung using the word in his introduction to the English translation of the *Book of Changes*, the *Yi Ching*. 'The matter of interest seems to be the configuration formed by chance events in the moment of observation,' Jung declared. There couldn't have been a neater description of the high which comes from smoking cannabis – and C. was nowadays on a permanent high, without needing drugs to get him there. Throwing the yarrow stalks C. was guided to the hexagram *meng* –

> *Youthful madness prospers.*
> *Not I seek the young madman.*
> *The young madman seeks me.*
> *With the first oracle, I give enlightenment.*
> *If he asks again, it is a trouble.*
> *If he makes trouble, I give no enlightenment.*
> *Persistence is rewarded.*

C. went away for a few days to an island in the Strait of

Georgia, north of Vancouver, to stay with people who would turn out to be future relatives of his. It was peaceful and remote, populated mostly by migrants from the madding crowd who had set up little cottage industries where they manufactured worry-beads and stained-glass windows. The people C. was staying with were not migrants but locals, a generation older than him. She ran the local post office; he fished for salmon in the Strait and told tall stories about his exploits with the OSS in the Second World War and his encounters with grizzly bears in the Yukon.

They drove a couple of miles from the house to show C. a fifteen-acre plot of land leading down to the beach where they were going to build a new home. The views across the Strait were magnificent.

'Fresh water's been the main problem,' said the teller of tall stories. 'I had to dowse for it, to see if there were sufficient underground sources for our needs.'

He went away and came back with a forked hazel twig. Holding it, he walked a few paces until the twig pointed downwards.

'Water!' he said proudly.

C. snickered.

'Here, I'll show you.'

He made C. hold the stick by the Y-fork in two hands, flexing it gently outwards while holding it horizontal. Feeling foolish, C. made several sweeps in the places he was shown, without success. Then the dowser made C. go back over the ground, this time putting his hands on C.'s shoulders. Before long the twig bent downwards, despite C.'s best efforts to hold it steady.

It had to be a trick, the kind of thing Uri Geller did with a spoon. C. didn't believe in the extra-sensory; he didn't even *want* to believe in it. In some annoyance he set off again on his own, holding the twig horizontally, as directed. As he walked across the dirt road alongside the cleared plot, the hazel twig came alive. It half-twisted out of C.'s tight grip and delivered a sharp blow to his left knee.

He pulled it up. It wanted to point down again. The teller of tall stories came up, delighted: C. had just walked over the place where the stream ran under the road. C. dropped the twig. He ran across the road and into the trees where the stream came out – and saw for himself that it was true.

He had no explanation. There is no accepted explanation for water-divining, other than that it appears to involve a physiological reflex within the dowser, reacting to some impulse from what he is dowsing for, or possibly sending out an impulse towards it. C. returned to Santa Cruz, shaken to the core. Nature was showing him things he had not known existed. It had waited until the defences of his reason were lowered before awarding him this privilege, to possess a sympathetic magic over its most precious creation.

He was becoming a child again, a child of nature. There is a beautiful passage in the third of his *Centuries of Meditations* in which the seventeenth-century English mystic Thomas Traherne describes the world he remembers seeing as a child –

'*All appeared new, and strange at first, inexpressibly rare and delightful and beautiful. I was a little stranger, which at my entrance into the world was saluted and surrounded with innumerable joys. My knowledge was Divine. I knew by intuition those things which, since my Apostasy, I collected again by highest reason. My every ignorance was advantageous. I seemed as one brought into the Estate of*

Innocence. *All things were spotless and pure and glorious: yea, and infinitely mine, and joyful and precious. I knew not that there were any sins, or complaints or laws. I dreamed not of poverties, contentions or vices. All tears and quarrels were hidden from my eyes. Everything was at rest, free and immortal. I knew nothing of sickness or death or rents or exaction, either for tribute or bread. In the absence of these I was entertained like an Angel with the works of God in their splendour and glory, I saw all in the peace of Eden; Heaven and Earth did sing my Creator's praises, and could not make more melody to Adam than to me. All Time was Eternity, and a perpetual Sabbath. Is it not strange, that an infant should be heir of the whole World, and see those mysteries which the books of the learned never unfold?'*

It fitted the frame of mind C. was in to put aside the book of Genesis and explore the notion that innocence is bliss. Ever since that moment in his grandfather's Methodist Church when he was unjustly compelled to tears, C. had rejected the central Christian message of sin and redemption and immersed himself instead in the beauty of holiness. At the school where he was educated, in the shadow of Canterbury Cathedral, he discovered that God could be represented by things which were beautiful and exhilarating rather than minatory. Instead of foursquare red brick, here were great stone shafts rising to an infinite tracery of fan-vaulting. The trumpeting organ and the pealing choir drowned out the miserable cries of penitent sinners. Gowned for Evensong in the Cathedral Undercroft, he watched the candle-light flicker on the Norman pillars and listened to the hushed responses and felt an ecstasy which was spiritual only in so far as things of beauty were spiritual.

Now, as then, C. was willing himself back into a state of innocence, like Traherne's, where such perceptions were possible. The essence of Paradise, he decided, must be associated with the deep instinct in us to identify the source of happiness with childhood, and to find in the innocence of our earliest recollections a purity which is like bliss and which we long to recapture.

Sigmund Freud found the longing for childhood happiness and unawareness of death to be so consistent in the unconscious life of his patients that he based his entire analytical method on its exposition. In our dreams we regress to the primitive mental patterns of our babyhood, he concluded: the period when our ego reigns supreme and we appear to possess the whole world around us. Our instincts too urge us back towards an earlier state of things, since, as he wrote in *Beyond the Pleasure-Principle*, 'It would be in contradiction to the conservative nature of our instincts if the goal of life were a state of things which had never been attained'.

In *Beyond the Pleasure-Principle*, Freud identified this earlier state with death. But according to his own theories about childhood, as some of Freud's disciples have pointed out since, a pre-ambivalent state also exists in infancy. Then too, as very young children, we experience that otherwise rare state of 'happy love' which Freud characterizes as 'the primal condition in which object-libido and ego-libido cannot be distinguished.'

Here, perhaps, was the true seat of Paradise – the child at his mother's breast, the lover at one with the loved. Eagerly seeking confirmation, C. checked out of the McHenry Library at UCSC a copy of *The Psychology of the Child*. Written by Jean Piaget, with the collaboration of Barbel

Inhalder, it summed up nearly fifty years of work in the field of child psychology, by its leading exponent.

Here was what C. was looking for – not an unknowing, but a knowledge surpassing anything the human brain can hope to grasp at in later life. He learned that after the total egocentrism of the twelve to eighteen-month-old baby there occurs a kind of gradual de-centring process whereby the young child comes to see himself as an object in a world made up of objects.

The de-centring normally takes five or six years. During this time the child is moving out of what Piaget calls a 'magical-phenomenalist' world in which everything that moves is assimilated to the child's own actions ('for instance many subjects between four and six believe that the moon follows them around or even that they force it to follow them'). During this period, writes Piaget, 'Names are at-tached physically to things; dreams are little material tableaus which you contemplate in your bedroom; thought is a kind of voice. *Animism* springs from the same lack of differentiation but in the opposite direction: everything that is in movement is alive and conscious, the wind knows that it blows, the sun that it moves, and so on.'

There is nothing new in the perception that children's lives are governed by their desires. Aristotle, arguing for the proper discipline of children, remarked that they are insatiable in pursuit of pleasure and draw their gratification from every quarter. In the nineteenth century it became a commonplace that the one refuge of fallen, sinful man was the paradise of childhood: shielded years of innocence and happiness before adolescence brought sexual guilt and an understanding of death's inevitability. But Piaget had taken a step further. He was confirming what Freud had deduced fifty years earlier, that as young children we live in a universe in which everything we see and touch is associated with the erotic impulses of our own bodies.

This infant state of 'happy love', in which self-love and outward-directed love are merged, is not a paradise theme taken up in modern literature. To find it described in detail, in terms astonishingly similar to those employed by twentieth-century psychologists, C. went back five centuries and more to the beatific visions of the Christian mystics.

The idea of mystical contemplation of the holy, as developed by St Augustine and other Church Fathers, actually dates back to the ancient Greeks. Aristotle had written that contemplation was the highest form of activity, bringing true happiness. Plato in the *Timaeus*, the one work of his which was around in St Augustine's day, had tried to explain what contemplation involved.

'Each man . . .' he wrote, 'by learning the harmonies and revolutions of the universe, *should assimilate the thinking being to the thought*, renewing his original nature, and having assimilated them should attain to that perfect life which the gods have set before mankind.'

No wonder the *Timaeus* was such a key text for the early Christian philosophers. Plato's disciple Plotinus, whose theories were as fashionable in St Augustine's era as Freud's in our own, wrote about the state of mystical trance. 'To see one must lose consciousness of oneself, and, to have consciousness of what is seen, one has to cease, to some extent, to see.' He goes on to explain, 'It is in this state of to-and-fro movement, of union and separation, that we develop a consciousness of the absorption of ourselves in the whole.'

This was how the Christian mystics would strive to see

God, by marshalling every faculty towards inward contemplation. The greatest of all medieval philosophers, St Thomas Aquinas, echoed Plotinus when he wrote that since we cannot hope to see God physically, it must be that God helps us to apprehend him in a different way. 'If God's essence is to be seen at all, it must be that the intellect sees it through the divine essence itself; so that in that vision the divine essence is both the object and the medium of vision.'

The goal of the Christian mystics and visionaries is very much the same as the Buddhist conception of nirvana. It is a state of oneness with God, an inward paradise, beyond care and worry, where they can rest happy in the knowledge that they are loved in the measure in which they love. Most of them saw this womb-paradise of exaltation – St Augustine's unutterable peace, the 'deep but dazzling darkness' of St John of the Cross – as the summit of their spiritual endeavour. Willing themselves back to the pre-rational state of the infant child, their mystical paradise was a progress through narcissism to an abandonment of self in an all-suffusing experience of Divinity.

The most glorious expression of this reciprocity between self-love and love comes in the final canto of Dante's *Paradiso*, as the poet, at the end of his journey, looks towards Christ-in-God –

> *Eternal light, that in Thyself alone*
> *Dwelling, alone dost know Thyself, and smile*
> *On Thy self-love, so knowing and so known!*
> *The sphering thus begot, perceptible*
> *In Thee like mirrored light, now to my view –*
> *When I had looked on it a little while –*
> *Seemed in itself, and in its own self-hue,*

Limned with our image; for which cause mine eyes
Were altogether drawn and held thereto.

            *   *   *

C. wrote a paper along these lines, describing how early
Christian accounts of mystical ecstasy and the modern
psychological studies of Freud and Piaget both led back to
the self-centred narcissism of childhood which lies behind
all that we know of Paradise. So far, so good. It was what
C. had set out to do, to get back to the source, the purest
place.

But he was still unsatisfied. At the moment in his own life
when he had come closest to his idea of Paradise, it was
receding from him.

Somehow, try as he would, innocence was not sustainable.
Not even with Laura. At first it seemed as if Robert's
knowledge of their love affair wasn't going to make any
difference. After he'd discovered Laura in bed with C. in
Spring Street, Robert, perversely, became much more cheer-
ful. He walked around like a man with a mystery disease
who has just been given a positive diagnosis. He found that
he could write again. He became almost sociable. He was
content, even, that Laura should go on seeing his rival (he
could hardly have stopped her). It was as if he had convinced
himself that, once C. was gone from Santa Cruz, Laura,
impressed by Robert's magnanimity, would come back to
him for good. The evil force would be exorcised that had
sucked her love away, and everything would be as it had
been in the beginning.

He said as much to C. when their paths crossed on campus, on C.'s way to play tennis, and Robert fell in with him.

'I'm going to let this thing run its course,' he announced.

'What?'

'No reason why you should know, but Laura's always been like this. Erratic. Impulsive. She has passions for things.' He looked C. up and down. 'They don't last, but there's no point in trying to stop her. She's very vulnerable.'

C. said nothing.

'I know why she fell for you,' Robert went on, after a pause.

'Oh? Do tell me.'

'Because of your height.'

C. stopped swinging his racket and looked at him sharply. But Robert was not the joky type.

'Yes. You're both about the same height. It is a well-attested fact that women are attracted to men who are on their eye-level. You don't know how lucky you are.'

'Do you really think so?'

'But you're going, anyway. Laura needs someone who's around, someone to look after her. She's very vulnerable. Letting you see her now is important for me to keep her trust. When you're gone we'll be fine again, the two of us.'

'Do you play tennis?' C. asked him as they stopped by the courts. Robert shook his head.

'I'm much too busy, I'm afraid.'

'A pity. It's very therapeutic,' C. said. 'See you around.'

Robert was saying the same things to Laura, of course . . . that there wasn't any future for her with C., that he was going back to England where he already had a lover. And Laura didn't have C.'s defences. He was going to leave – wasn't he? And if so, where was the point of her going on seeing him, when it would just make parting harder to bear?

Whatever strength and confidence Laura now had to deal with Robert, had been won at the cost of falling in love with C. It was as if she had been offered some Faustian pact – win your freedom and lose your soul. For C. it was turning out to be exactly the opposite. In loving Laura he felt that he had discovered his soul – but the price of keeping it would be to lose his freedom and stay in California.

Though Laura understood this, she never pressed him. She knew that it was a dilemma C. would have to resolve on his own. But C. didn't want to resolve it. As the summer wore on, browning the meadow grass and darkening the green leaf of the live-oak, he set aside his work on Paradise, for the time being, and started writing a story, based on a love affair he'd had in England some years before. Looking at it now, I observe that C., in transposing the situation to the West Coast, had altogether abandoned his sense of irony. The girl's worsening schizophrenia is transmuted into a romantic psychosis; her lover's pain and embarrassment becomes, in the story, a heroic determination that the reality of love should be more curative than anything pills and drugs can achieve. The weather is overheated too: inland and along the coast mysterious fires burn.

Love is all you need. Actually it doesn't turn out that way in the end. In real life, C. had walked out. In the story, the forces of repressive sanity separate the lovers, leaving the man distracted in the grip of his obsession. Putting C.'s manuscript down I noticed, with a sense of foreboding, that he had succeeded in shifting the blame, much as those fashionable gurus of 1960s psychoanalysis used to do. In

C.'s notebook I found a quotation, chillingly facile, from Dr R. D. Laing – 'Sanity or psychosis is tested by the degree of conjunction or disjunction between two persons where the one is sane by common consent.'

Love is all you need. How C. wished, all the same, that that were true. Like Faust dicing with the impossible, he would have given anything for time to stand still. So would Laura: but for her Santa Cruz was no effortless interlude eight thousand miles from home. Right here was her life, her career, her world. It wasn't possible any longer to sustain the fiction that in Arcadia, in Eden, love carries no responsibility. C.'s paradise was about to be put to the test.

2

The steam shrouding the Atlantic far below told me I was approaching my destination. It marked the area of ocean where the ice-cold waters of the Labrador current meet the warm waters of the Gulf Stream curving eastwards towards Europe, off the coast of Nova Scotia. The 747 would shortly be beginning its descent.

A few months had gone by. I'd been back in London, catching up with my life. I'd left C. in his self-enclosed Eden and knew that I had to go back: but I still needed to locate Jan and Hélène – especially Hélène. In the meantime I transcribed my tapes and looked at the notes I'd assembled. I wrote my weekly book reviews for the newspaper. The phone in my office rang with ideas for screenplays that would never get made. My wife finished the biography she was working on and started dealing in antiques. Our son came home from school and played football with his friends in the garden. People came to dinner; I opened the wine and made the coffee, and couldn't concentrate on what they were saying.

I needed to drag the past into the present, somehow. I had gone back across a bridge of years to a time before marriage, house, mortgage, child, job, routine, all the concomitants of growing older which fix us in a mould and limit our opportunities to break out, assume some new and different identity. In going back and immersing myself in this earlier time I had cracked the mould of whatever I had hardened into – not enough to break free, but enough to make me feel restless and vulnerable. Incomplete.

Something was missing. But I didn't know where to go looking for it. What Andrea had said kept coming back and haunting me. I thought of the incomparable beauty and peace of her rooms in Topside and then of a .22 snub-nose revolver kept somewhere in a drawer like a curled snake . . . it seemed to stand for all the darker knowledge of which C. had been ignorant, that summer.

And then one day, going through an old desk I had taken down to the country, I found a little black book, lying under a sheaf of postcards. It was C.'s diary for 1976. I flicked through it. The Chicago months were packed with details of his engagements. Drinks, squash, an Arts Club opening, dinner with friends, the Chicago Symphony. The California months were empty. Page after page of blank days, topped and tailed by a curt itinerary of the journey out and the journey back. If I needed proof that C.'s months in Spring Street had been lived outside calendar time, here it was in front of me. I skimmed through to the back.

And discovered the breakthrough I had been looking for.

Names. Names and telephone numbers, a host of them. Some I didn't recognize any more. Who was Don Nicholl? Tom Cartelli? Barry Katz? Zen McClane? Who was Roberta, whom C. had known well enough not to bother with her surname? But among them were the two names I needed in full. Hélène McDougall. Jan Furniss. Telephone numbers too, not that I expected them to be of any use, thirteen years on. Except that, beside Hélène's name and address C. had scribbled another name – *c/o Martha Dumas*. Vaguely I remembered Hélène telling me about the woman she described as her surrogate mother. I picked up the phone and dialled the Idyllwild number. A woman answered.

'Hallo. I'm trying to reach Martha Dumas.'

'This is she.'

I thought about what Andrea had said. My throat constricted. What if Hélène was dead? I gabbled something about who I was, and how I came to be looking for this old friend of mine, Helen McDougall, whom I had shared a house with years ago in Santa Cruz. Was she . . . did she know how I could get in touch?

A pleasant voice answered me. Helen was alive and well. She had her ups and downs but basically she was okay. She'd got her BA in French Literature and lived in Boulder for a good while. She'd met somebody and moved with him to Los Angeles, but hated LA, 'as you can imagine'. Now she lived in Canada –

In *Canada* –

In Halifax, Nova Scotia. In a Buddhist community in Halifax, Nova Scotia. Her name now was Hélène Rameshwan. Would I like her address?

I put down the phone and poured myself a drink. Then I wrote to Hélène Rameshwan in Halifax. *Dear Hélène, You probably won't remember me . . . I'm stopping off in Halifax, as it happens, on my way back to London, and if you happen to be around . . .*

The seat-belt signs came on. I scrabbled around in the airline bag, and found what I was looking for.

Dear Christopher
What a surprise it was to receive your letter! Yes, I do remember you – it really was like lifetimes ago. I would be delighted if you dropped in around the time you say. I look forward to talking with you again.

I'd better get this off to you, since you are planning
your trip.
À bientôt j'espère
Hélène.

Her given name was Helen, she'd confided to C. in Spring Street, but that was one of the many things from her past she preferred to jettison. The name Hélène was European and Europe was her goal: its culture, its mystique. That was why she was studying French. That was the reason for Boris, her Swiss-Russian boyfriend.

C. was sitting on the sun-terrace, his Olympia typewriter on the table, and Hélène had come to sit beside him on the bleached wooden bench as she often did, to sunbathe and gossip and read her book. Auburn-haired, with large dark eyes, a snub nose and a pointed chin, she looked like Tuesday Weld in one of her early beach-picnic movies. She wore a pair of shorts, nothing else, and stretched her legs out under the table. She was in her second year at college.

C.'s typing was suddenly full of spelling mistakes. He cursed and changed paper.

'Don't you think you should have gone on with Paradise?' Hélène asked him.

'My story is about a kind of Paradise. At least in the beginning. It becomes different and darker when the girl gets ill. But it's like Heaven and Hell. Paradise doesn't make sense without some sort of background of tragedy.'

'Oh. I guess not. I think it's great that you can write a story about love, and passion. I would not know where to begin!'

I suppose that was one of several occasions when C. could have asked Hélène what she meant, and she might have told him something of her history which would have changed his impression of her as a sweet, childlike girl who was earnestly trying out lifestyles, like so many Baskin-Robbins icecreams. But something must have caught her attention at that point – possibly it was Lowrie come out to weed the vegetable garden – and Hélène jumped up and left him to his story.

C. knew that there must have been some childhood unhappiness because Hélène avoided all contact with her family in Los Angeles. But a lot of people have childhood troubles. What was memorable about Hélène was her bouncy exuberant friendliness, her wide-eyed openness and emotionalism. She radiated earnestness – about sex, for instance. It wasn't as wonderful, she told C., as her reading of books had led her to believe. This was presumably the responsibility of Boris, her Russian pianist boyfriend who had turned up at Spring Street out of the blue.

Boris, egotistical and vain, didn't seem to be doing Hélène much good. But it would be unfair to blame him for one of the most frightening moments of C.'s life. C. was sitting reading on his bed in the alcove. There was suddenly a piercing scream, not more than a few yards away from where he sat. He leapt to his feet. The scream died away in a strangulated noise and was followed by another ear-shattering scream as if a woman was fighting off a maniac who was stabbing her to death. The sound came from Hélène's room. C. raced over; he . . . knocked on the door. Silence. Then the door opened; Hélène stood there. Her face was flushed, her eyes were wet, but she seemed unhurt. In fact she had an anxious smile on her face.

'Hi!' she said. 'Does my therapy bother you? I didn't know anybody was around.'

Primal screaming, to relieve frustration, was just one of the many pseudo-therapeutic fads going the rounds in 1976, along with Rolfing, rebirthing, orgonomy and transactional analysis. Hélène liked to pick up on these things; far from fearing for her sanity, C. didn't give it a second thought. He might have stopped to consider that primal screaming was more psycho than analysis. Arthur Janov, whose primal therapy was established to help people act out and resolve the buried pain of childhood, had been reported as saying 'I believe the only way to eliminate neurosis is with overthrow by force and violence.'

But C. didn't know any of this. As far as he was concerned, Hélène was getting out her feelings about Boris, or about Howard, who bawled her out when she missed one of her household rotas, or Rick, who sometimes snapped at her when she left her dirty dishes in the sink, or herself for not losing weight fast enough. In any case it didn't seem to do Hélène any harm. There would be this hideous, breast-beating wail climaxing in floods of hysterical sobbing . . . and the next day she'd be out happily sunbathing in the orchard or chattering away to me on the sun-terrace while the breeze off Monterey Bay brought with it the scent of yellow roses from the garden.

The road from the airport cut through a thick-pile carpet of green conifers. Rocky-islanded lakes with summer chalets were visible through the trees. Without any of the roadside sprawl of American towns, Halifax suddenly introduced itself in polite rows of pastel weatherboarded houses and bungalows set in neatly swept lots. Apart from the Crazy Horse Cabaret, proudly presenting from the USA centrefold

Janie Frickie in *The Dating Game*, I might have been in Scandinavia. But this was Nova Scotia, where Hélène was now living in her Buddhist community – about as far from California as she could have travelled on the North American continent.

I had no telephone number for her. Just an address, in a street which wasn't marked on my map of Halifax. It was evening; I was too tired to start driving around town. I ate some dinner and went back to my hotel room to read Bruno Bettelheim's *The Uses of Enchantment*. One passage caught my eye. I was to go back to it, later, with increased respect.

'*I have known many examples where, particularly in late adolescence, years of belief in magic are called upon to compensate for the person's having been deprived of it prematurely in childhood . . . Many young people who today suddenly seek escape in drug-induced dreams, apprentice themselves to some guru, believe in astrology, engage in practising "black magic", or who in some other fashion escape from reality into daydreams about magic experiences which are to change their lives for the better, were prematurely pressed to view reality in an adult way.*'

It was an unshowy, blue-painted, foursquare clapboard house like all the others in Preston Street, standing in a small yard. An external wooden staircase led up to two apartments on the upper floor. Pinned up on her front door was a note to remind Hélène to purchase Soft Skin flea-remover for the dog. I rang the bell. There was no immediate answer, except for a shrill yapping. Then the door opened, as it had done that first day in Spring Street, and a woman who was the exact image of Hélène leaned forward through the doorway and gave me a shy peck on the cheek.

She was taller and more heavily built than I had
remembered, and wearing a long green and mauve dress
that must have been mothballed since the late 1950s. Moving
with a stately, almost matronly gait she took me inside to
where a small, scruffy, white rug on four feet nuzzled my
ankles before climbing back on the chair.

'His name's Tachi,' she said with a bright, nervous laugh.
'Tachi, get down off that chair!' She bent awkwardly and
scooped Tachi on to the floor. She had beautiful hands. I
sat down. 'He's a Lhasa Apso,' she said. 'Do you know
them? They come from Tibet.'

It was a young girl's voice still – not quite in control,
hitting all the notes of the register. If it wasn't for the dress,
and the care with which Hélène moved around, making
coffee, lowering herself down on to the sofa, I'd have said
she hadn't changed at all – the same auburn hair and large,
dark pleading eyes, the same elfin look, the same tense
vulnerability. The apartment was stuffy, claustrophobic,
womblike, made smaller by the heavy, awkward furniture.
It, too, had a fifties feel. She sat in it, day after day, waiting
for her husband Samphal to come up from Los Angeles
where he had work as a computer programmer. She visited
with her Buddhist friends in Halifax; she took Tachi for
walks; on good days she drove down to the empty coastline
and looked at the waves crashing on the rocks. Mostly she
sat in the apartment while Samphal Rameshwan sorted his
life out in California and they waited to hear about their
applications for work permits.

It was a strange, lonely life. Now in her early thirties
Hélène had cut herself adrift, or perhaps she had been adrift
from the beginning . . . She'd stayed on in Spring Street for
a few months after I left and then had gone for a year to

Aix en-Provence. It was in France that she had picked up on an interest in Buddhism which had begun in her first year at UCSC, when she'd attended a class in Archaic Consciousness with Norman O. Brown – 'a bit of Hinduism, Buddhism, all the kinds of things I was really interested in'. Back in Santa Cruz in late 1977 she'd done a couple of semesters of religious studies. But the Buddhist teaching was dry and academic, not inspirational, so she switched back to French Literature and developed her Buddhism by joining a Dharma Study Group in her spare time.

After Santa Cruz she began having trouble with her health. For six months she lived in New York City with a boyfriend. The apartment was infested with cockroaches and was intensively sprayed with a roach poison which, it turned out, affected human nerve-ends. When she could stand it no longer, she left New York and went to a Buddhist meditation centre outside Washington DC.

She went on from there to Boulder, Colorado, for her Buddhist initiation, during which she met her Indian husband Samphal, another Buddhist. For some years she stayed in Boulder and taught French. It was then that she began to suffer from the rheumatoid arthritis which still afflicted her and which was the cause of the stately deliberateness I'd noticed in the way she moved. Then as now she needed peace and quiet; the pain flared up and crippled her when she was under pressure. She gave up teaching. Her Tibetan guru, Tru Paribachay, moved up to Nova Scotia two years before he died, and she followed him. Halifax was a good area for Buddhism to flourish, so the guru had said.

'There's a feeling of restfulness in Halifax,' said Hélène, her hands on her knees, her back straight. 'People just aren't going anywhere fast. The level of aggression you feel in the States isn't happening here; it makes a big difference in the atmosphere. There's a basis of goodness here: you feel you could take care of *life* in a good way.'

I nodded. I understood what she was saying. What I wanted to know was – *Why?* Hélène had a book beside her. With one hand on the arm of the sofa she got up and gave it to me. It was called *The Myth of Freedom and the Way of Meditation*, by Chogyam Trungpa.

I read aloud from the back jacket – 'Freedom is generally conceived as the ability to achieve goals and satisfy desires. But what of the source of these goals and desires? If they arise from ignorance, habitual patterns and negative emotions – in other words from psychologically destructive elements that actually enslave us – is the freedom to pursue them true freedom or just a myth?'

So Hélène told me about her childhood.

She grew up in suburban Pennsylvania, with a mother who preferred the bottle to her youngest daughter. She had every excuse for taking to drink. Her other two children, much older than Hélène, had both been thalidomide babies. Her first husband, whom she loved, had died of lung cancer at the age of thirty. Hélène was the child of her second marriage, to the gas station attendant at the bottom of the street. Hélène didn't remember him. He had died when she was five years old. For six years in Pennsylvania Hélène bore the brunt of her mother's alcoholic misery. Then she too died. Hélène, an eleven-year-old orphan, was shunted about between relatives like a boat on the ocean and eventually ended up living with her elder sister Sally in Los Angeles.

An extraordinary Cinderella existence lay in store for

her. Sally, aged twenty-three, was divorced, with two children aged three and five. There was no money. The family was on welfare, which in Los Angeles is worse than having a criminal record. Sally the thalidomide victim had just one arm; the other was hardly more than an excrescence. Embittered by what Hélène called 'her feeling of un-wholeness', she was nevertheless determined to succeed.

She got a job, with her one arm, at the Shadowlight Club in Beverly Hills, and became a call-girl. Every day at home she would get up late and put on her make-up and single-mindedly set about the job of pursuing rich men. In the middle of shouting at the kids and bawling out Hélène for not keeping them quiet, the phone would ring. Sally would answer it with an affected '*Oh hallo!*' and that would be the last they would see of her until the following day. Hélène, not yet in her teens, was left alone in the house to raise the two children.

'Unfortunately there was so much cruelty in the home, because there was just total aggression towards the children and towards myself – because she didn't want to be burdened down, she wanted to be a single person. She'd been alone with them, and this ex-husband who would ring her up and say I'm coming over with a gun to kill you and, you know, regularly threatening her life . . . she needed to pass that aggression on to someone else in the family. So she'd say to me – "I want you to clean the house up, here's some speed!" or, "I want you to cool down, here's some Valium." She was really into pills!'

Hélène was smiling wryly, but her voice was brittle with the pain of her story. There had been no more love in that Los Angeles household than there had been in

Pennsylvania. The children were miserable and screamed a lot. For five years, until she was sixteen, Hélène got home from her public school and cooked their lunch and their dinner and cleaned up the house and put them to bed.

'I was pretty much their mother. Mainly, I wasn't free to go out. It was a very unbalanced life. Really scary. And I still feel to this very day, Christopher, that I need to learn how to nurture myself – you know what I'm saying?'

Her sister Sally's dream came true. Against all the odds, she found herself a millionaire and married him. By that time Hélène had made her break for freedom. At sixteen, she won a scholarship to a private school in the mountains. Her French teacher there was a kindly, middle-aged woman – Martha Dumas. For the first time Hélène was given the affection and nurturing which she had been looking for all her life.

'She was somebody I idolized and whom I love tremendously, I love her like a mother, even though it can never be the same thing. I spent my vacations with her. Introducing me, she used to say, "This is my daughter."'

Her French teacher! The pieces began to fit into place. Hélène associated Europe with love, and love with Europe. Perhaps that had been the reason for Boris.

'Who?'

'Boris.'

'Ohhh!'

'You'd forgotten about Boris?' I burst out laughing. Hélène joined in, rocking back in embarrassment.

'Oh my God! That boyfriend you mean! Russian,

the Russian pianist! His family was very wealthy; he didn't have to do anything for a living. Oh my God, and Alexis! His cousin Alexis who I really had the crush on!'

I said that I'd never heard Boris play the piano, or speak Russian for that matter.

'He didn't even have a piano at home! I was living with him in Lausanne and he didn't possess a piano, that I recall!'

She had gone to see him in Switzerland during her year at Aix and had spent some days touring with him in the Alps, shivering on the pillion of his motorcycle. That was when, she said, things between them fell apart.

'Well, it was fun, you know! He was a true European, that fellow. A real eccentric. A lot of the aristocratic White Russian pretence, but a bit of a cold fish. I think it was just mainly that I was at the phase when I was so impressionable . . .' She raised her eyebrows coyly. 'That was my European fling!'

The rug raised a leg and started scratching itself. Hélène fussed over it – 'Oh, honey, don't do that!' – and we decided to go out for a walk, on which Hélène would be able to buy the Soft Skin flea-remover. The rug rolled around excitedly. Hélène attached a lead to it and we went down the back stairs into the street. Despite the warm stillness of the afternoon, the streets of Halifax were almost deserted. Like a retired couple we promenaded slowly down the road and into the park, Hélène telling me that when she went to the market she made as many friends through Tachi as other people make through their children. She wasn't yet ready to be a mother again. Tachi was the substitute.

'I have to keep bathing him, and putting on flea powder,' she said fondly. 'There are so many fleas here.'

We bought sandwiches and sat down in the park to eat them. It all seemed a million miles away from Spring Street. That, plainly, was what Hélène intended. There was nothing left for her in California except bad memories: even of Topside. She had come back from Europe and tried to reclaim one of the spare rooms, and Howard and Rick had decided to rent it to Rose Seeger's sister instead. For a while, Hélène slept down in the alcove where C. had been. The little room she used to have ('it was sixty dollars a month — so cheap!') was being used as storage. When she wanted it back, she said, Howard did a number on her — 'and that really jangled my nerves and I had to leave.'

'What do you mean?'

She took a deep breath. 'Well frankly, you know, he had the power. Like saying, "Well we'll give you a room or we won't give you a room, it just depends on whether you do what I want you to do." And that was too heavy, so . . .' Hélène arched her eyebrows.

'And he made it all quite clear?'

'Yeah, pretty much. It was pretty definite.' She must have sensed my disbelief, because she began talking about Howard and his house rules.

'Things had to be done, you know, *on the spot*,' she clicked her fingers, '*right now*,' another click, 'and they had to be exact. You never ever left a dish dirty, or Howard would come after you with the stick, practically! If you could accept his authority, then there was enough space. But if you didn't accept it, or you bucked it, then you were *out*, because he ran things.'

She laughed nervously, a little girl's laugh. 'He isn't going to come after me now, is he?'

Rick, Katie, Jan, Lowrie . . . she remembered them, but not willingly. And the primal screaming she had completely forgotten. She gave one of her soundless, mouth-agape laughs, rocking back at the thought – 'You mean – did you *hear* it?' Like all the other things she tried back in 1976 'when everybody was trying to be free', she didn't think it had helped her much.

What she missed about Spring Street was what everyone else missed, what I'd got used to hearing from all of them: the special way the sun shone in through the high windows, the position of the house between sea and mountain with its majestic view over Monterey Bay – 'and you had the gardens of heaven around you, really resplendent, with flowers blooming all the time, and grass in the orchard where we used to sit down'. She thought of them, like Laura, as English gardens in a Californian sun.

And Andrea. Hélène loved Andrea second only to Martha Dumas, it seemed to me. 'I was always in there, you know, in those rooms; she didn't mind, it was the best place to be. And Rafiki! I loved Rafiki, he was so brave and beautiful. I used to look after him when Andrea went away, until he died.'

'Rafiki died?'

'He was dying of leukaemia all that time. Getting thinner and thinner. Didn't Andrea tell you?'

I shook my head. I thought of Hélène, the way Andrea had described her, a frightened bird seeking a refuge. She had escaped from Los Angeles into the mountains, and then to Santa Cruz, but the inner desolation she hadn't escaped.

She'd grown up with people, as she told me, who had lost any kind of perspective on what was important, outside of getting famous and rich and looking good, and she was in profound disagreement with those values without knowing where or how to get values of her own. Now she could look back and feel sorry for her sister's children, the boy and girl she'd brought up until she was sixteen, 'because they've adopted those exact same materialistic values, they've come out as typical Los Angeles types, really superficial, they don't care about people ... I wish there was some way I could help, that I could have been there for those kids. But at the same time I couldn't help myself, I had to find my own path.'

Which was what she was attempting to do in Santa Cruz when she knew C. thirteen years ago – trying to find a path. Somehow she'd found a way through to this terminus on the other edge of North America, and it hadn't yet led her to a safe haven; she was still struggling against fate. Six months she had been here, and Samphal was still in Los Angeles as he had been for the past year, occasionally coming up to visit. He wasn't due to come and see her again for a couple of months. Good and gentle as she evidently was, Hélène felt her husband's absence with as near to bitterness as she ever came. Last night she'd rung him and talked of flying down to see him in LA. To which Samphal had replied – Don't do anything silly, you should know better, LA would *really* crack you up.

There'd been an awkward pause when she told me this. It was now evening; Hélène had insisted on taking me to meet her Buddhist friends, her link with the outside world. In a tall Victorian room with polished floorboards Gary and Sandy, Don and Marilyn, Hélène and myself, sat round on chairs with plates on our knees, eating a supper which Sandy and Marilyn had prepared (Hélène was eating macrobiotic). Hospitable, open and friendly, they plainly felt a deep protectiveness towards her as well as a real tenderness. In this small circle, the only one she knew, Hélène was like a child again, chattering and laughing, talking about her translating work and the French teaching she did when her health permitted it ('there's so much bilingualism here, I watch French TV all the time!') and about Samphal who never came, and the long drives she took out into the country . . . and I saw them watching her affectionately and felt their almost tangible anxiety.

She had said to me at some point earlier in the day, sitting forward in her green and mauve dress and speaking in a confidential tone, that the thing which had been most beneficial to her in all of life had been seeing and associating with people who had kind hearts and open minds, because that had released her from the suffering, the psychological poverty, of her earlier years. I didn't know what to say. C. had misjudged her once; I didn't want to misjudge her now. She had been hurt too much not to need to trust people, and yet she trusted people too much not to end up being hurt by them.

At the end of the evening I kissed Hélène goodbye and wished her well. Very early the next morning, my notebooks packed, my job done, I drove to the airport and caught the plane to San Francisco.

*   *   *

I needed still to find Jan Furniss, the other sophomore who'd been in Spring Street. Her surname had turned up in C.'s 1976 diary too late for me to check her out at UCSC. Something Rick had said about her had stayed with me. According to Rick, Jan had become even more politically radicalized after C. had left. He wasn't sure that she'd even bothered to graduate from UCSC.

At the airport I hired a car and headed south. There was some research work I had to do on a film project, so after booking into a nearby motel I stopped off at Stanford University and went to look at some papers in the Hoover Institute. At five o'clock the doors closed. Tired and hungry, I went back to the car and drove away. It was on one of the narrow paved roads that crosses campus, Stanford chapel on my right, the other side of some playing fields, that it happened.

Something extraordinary.

A sickening noise, like the grinding of giant teeth, rose up from beneath my feet. I lost control of the steering. The car wandered and floated across the road and then sank, as though all four tyres had punctured simultaneously.

Or so I thought, but I was wrong, because just as I was pulling in to the side of the road (nothing behind me or in front, thank God) the tyres recovered, in fact seemed to swell to an enormous size, as if they were about to burst. And still the giant teeth were grinding.

This time I pulled over and stopped, the sweat breaking out on my forehead. I'd had an eight-hour journey from London. I'd had nothing to eat since somewhere over Chicago, and I'd gone straight into a library to scrutinize documents and cuttings under a desklamp for the past three hours. There was nothing wrong with the car . . . it was me, my head was swimming, I needed to get some food inside me and take things easy.

Gingerly, I started the car and drove off campus. Directly opposite the main gates, across US 280, was Stanford shopping mall. I drove in and parked the car, and went looking for something to eat.

The mall was closed. Or rather, the shops were open but no one was serving. A few people were standing around, talking quietly. When I asked to see a menu they looked at me in shock and shook their heads.

I was getting desperate. I couldn't risk driving in this state. I'd had another brief dizzy spell, nearly losing my balance just as I got out of the car. A few cops had turned up and were listening in on their radio telephones. Now I noticed, some of the shops had their windows smashed. Groceries and books had been hurled around the floor. I guessed that a gang of kids must have run through, ransacking the sales areas, but was that any reason for closing down the whole mall?

Feeling like someone in a bad dream, I tottered back to the car. A middle-aged man was in the car next to mine. He didn't seem to be going anywhere; he was just sitting there. He looked up at me, his face drained, his voice unsteady.

'That was one hell of a shaker,' he said.

Shaker?

Earthquake?

Everything slid back into focus. The bad dream was over. I may have been the last person in the Bay Area to realize that I'd been in an earthquake which hit 7.1 on the Richter scale. For sure I was the only one to respond with a feeling of profound relief.

Christopher Hudson

In the immediate, dazed aftermath there was a long moment when the rest of the world went about its business as though nothing had happened. As I drove to the motel, the one local radio station to stay on air, in Santa Clara, was still carrying commercials for a big sale of porcelain in downtown San Jose. That would now be broken porcelain. Although Palo Alto and Stanford had escaped the worst damage, the big lamp on my motel-room bedside table was on the floor several feet away. The power was cut, in any case. I went back out and sat in the car for the next couple of hours, monitoring the radio.

Even then it took time for the seriousness of the quake to filter through. Calls came in to the radio station: shocked voices reporting fires, roads closed, bookshelves fallen over, cracks in the plaster. The Santa Clara newscasters were trying valiantly to piece the jigsaw together and separate fact from rumour. Fires in the Marina district of San Francisco – *fact*. The University library at Berkeley on fire – *rumour*. News that a fifty-foot section of the Bay Bridge had collapsed on to the lower freeway – rumour, surely, please God, *the Bay Bridge*, but no, it was true. Reports of widespread damage coming in from the mountain towns north of Santa Cruz near where the epicentre of the quake had been – *fact*.

Nevertheless all this time, as I listened to the car radio in the black-out, almost no casualties were reported. The main anxieties expressed on air were whether or not to turn the gas off, and whether schools would open in the morning, and how best to preserve unrefrigerated food. I went to bed without knowing or suspecting that between Marin County and Watsonville two thousand people had been injured and nearly one hundred lay dead or dying, most of them crushed under the concrete of the Nimitz Freeway in Oakland, after the second most powerful earthquake in the history of the United States.

I awoke to the noise of a helicopter. The TV had switched on during the night and was relaying scenes of the Marina district still burning in the grey dawn light. Then came pictures of the Cypress section of the Nimitz Freeway and the rescuers bringing out bodies. I called home to reassure my near-hysterical family in England who had been getting reports that half of San Francisco lay devastated. Then I phoned round to check how the others were, the people that I'd come to see.

Andrea, back from her field trip to Africa, I was supposed to be having lunch with. I couldn't get through to her at all. Howard and Tessa weren't answering their phone either, but there had been no reports of damage from the Oakland Hills. I called up Laura, who had written to say that she had got her doctorate and had moved with Jim to a house in Aptos, east of Santa Cruz. To my relief the phone rang, and Laura answered it. Barely ten miles from the epicentre they were still getting regular aftershocks and had shifted everything to the ground floor; but unlike some in Aptos they'd suffered no structural damage.

Finally I got through to Katie Tellier. She had been underground on one of San Francisco's trans-Bay tube trains when the quake hit – the last place on earth I'd have wanted to be. Fortunately the tunnel rode out the shaking. None of the passengers knew what had happened, until Katie walked up the stilled escalator and found herself emerging into an eerily darkened city with dust hanging in the air and the horizon lit with flames from the burning Marina district.

She walked home in the dust and darkness and began picking things up off the kitchen floor.

The death toll was rising, although in the best American spirit the newscasters concentrated on the upside . . . motorists brought out miraculously alive from their crushed vehicles; a Transit bus with forty passengers on the Bay Bridge which had somehow managed to pull up safely within seven feet of the collapsed section. They could have added – something that I saw for myself during the first twenty-four hours – that the people of the Bay Area had a great deal to pride themselves on, and not just the resilience of their earthquake-conscious architecture. The back-up services swung into action with an efficiency and kindly practicality which would have done credit to Londoners in the Blitz. Everybody was in on it, from local residents taking hot food and drink to the homeless, to the TV and radio stations wiping their schedules to act as clearing-houses for information, to the small electronics company making a free gift to the police of five hundred radio telephones and the brewery turning over one of its lines to distributing bottled water.

This wasn't the California I'd been writing about, the flaky, lotus-eating society I'd briefly been a part of in 1976. That existed, still exists: but I was being confronted wherever I looked with the other side, the one that doesn't fit the preconceptions of Easterners. When I went to see Andrea in her rustic cottage in Berkeley she found out that I was on my way down to Santa Cruz and insisted on taking me round the back to a shed at the bottom of the garden. Inside were all the toys her six-year-old son Oliver had grown out of. Together we hauled them out and washed them and put them in shopping bags in the trunk of my car, along with some old clothes Andrea turned up, so that I could take them to whatever Santa Cruz charity was coordinating earthquake relief.

I told Andrea about Stanford and the road suddenly turning into a waterbed. She described going round and comforting her seventy-three-year-old mother a few miles south from us who'd been badly shaken by the quake, and by the building in flames just a block away. I'd set out this time, as I've said, to find some means of dragging the past into the present day and here it was all around the two of us in dust and shattered buildings and snaking yellow gas lines, a present as well as a past that we suddenly had in common.

Although, as it now dawned on me, of all the Spring Street people I had met, Andrea's was the life least changed. We sat in her bungalow surrounded by things I recognized – the valuable African carvings and fabrics, the rattan furniture, the beaded Masai mats on the table, the cats, including the ancient, stately and irritable Attico, aged eighteen and a half, the younger sister of the famous Rafiki. She was teaching the same knowledge to the same kind of students as she had done in Santa Cruz. She was coping with their problems, as she had coped with Hélène's and Jan's. The chief difference was being got ready, unwillingly, for school – Oliver, a very good-looking six-year-old with long black curly hair, her son by a United Nations official.

All this while Andrea had succeeded in keeping her space in the world, that precious freedom of action and commitment which all of us had taken for granted when we were young. But talking to her this time, it was clear that Andrea too was approaching a watershed. Under President Reagan, the values of California's ultra-conservative Orange County had spread across the whole state. The life Andrea had made for herself was built on a radicalism which was increasingly hard to sustain. Even so she had no plans to give up teaching, though she sometimes thought of going to live in Amsterdam, where her brother was a senior executive of Friends of the Earth. Meanwhile she was hoping that the expense of her African field trips wouldn't mean that she would have to sell this cottage we were in – its Victorian clutter of rugs, pictures and furniture co-existing as contentedly as the cat curled up on a cushion in the corner.

Her life in Spring Street, she said, had grown into a kind of melancholy, finishing phase. (She had left the house for good a year after C. did.) In 1977 her UCSC college, Kresge, which more than any of the others had been run as a radical collective (faculty meetings took the form of encounter groups), was being taken over by administrators. All over the university people were leaving. Women's Studies, which Andrea had helped start at UCSC, was gradually run down. 'The collective structure was over . . . and that, you know, was my life.'

She had thought a lot about our meeting in the spring at the Ariel Café, and the significance I placed on the past. It had made her decide to write a serious autobiographical novel, which would fictionalize a life story that was extraordinary by any standard. It began with a Chicago childhood of broken homes and broken marriages.

After university and her graduate programme – six months in the African bush with nomadic tribesmen, six months in a southside Chicago ghetto – she had come to Santa Cruz and ended up with her brother renting a deserted

British clubhouse, ringed with palm trees, overlooking Monterey Bay, at the end of a road in Capitola. Here she finished her doctorate, on the origins of famine, and threw herself into anti-War politicking, organizing demonstrations and coordinating state-wide meetings.

It was a time when the clash of cultures was at its most extreme, and the friction manifested itself in any number of bizarre ways. One of Andrea's colleagues at the University, Maria, fell in with a couple of radicals who had written a successful book attempting to fuse linguistic theory and psychology into a form of psychotherapy – but its effects on the two of them were anything but therapeutic. They talked incessantly about the techniques of power, and violence, and the significance of violence. It wasn't all that long ago that Ed Kemper had been convicted of ten serial killings, many of them young West Coast students including the child of one of Maria's friends. Now two of her students were found dead; nobody was to discover the murderer.

Eventually the FBI ran Andrea out of the Capitola clubhouse, which was when she moved into the A-frame at the end of a mountain gulch in Aptos, among the redwoods and madrones.

It was lonely, in the forest up at the end of the dirt road, with no link to civilization except a battered mailbox and one telephone wire. Andrea bought the .22 snubnose and learned how to use it. She had an affair, which broke up violently. The man emptied her bank account and stole her Mazda, before moving out and leaving her more alone than ever, in what she described as 'a death house' – 'that little redwood A-frame, you could just kick the door open'.

'It was such a sick phase, up there,' Andrea said. 'The people I knew had something going that was very weird, very bizarre. It's quite frightening to me, when I think back on my relationships at that time. And you know, Christopher, I have almost never had truly vicious thoughts towards someone, but I used actually to dream of this man's plane going down.'

It was now three in the morning. Everything was quiet. Even the cats had long since gone to sleep. Andrea had made up a divan bed for me in Oliver's room; in a few hours' time I would be heading south to Santa Cruz. I fell asleep, but dreams woke me in the darkness before dawn.

So this was the violence which Andrea had mentioned in the Ariel Café – an ugly distillation of the Vietnam War and mysticism and power therapies. The clouds were rolling in above my Eden. Wherever I went there were intimations of death and viciousness. I'd recently heard a rumour that members of the Manson family had lived for a while up in the hills above Santa Cruz, before they moved south to Los Angeles in 1969 and massacred Sharon Tate and her friends in Polanski's house on Cielo Drive.

I should have anticipated something like this. Santa Cruz County was too beautiful not to lend itself to mystical fantasies. It attracted gamblers, clairvoyants, voodoo worshippers, cultists and fanatics of every description, all seeking some utopian solution inspired by the loveliness of the surroundings. This place gave the lie to Keats: beauty and truth were not inseparable. Nor did the mind necessarily rise to higher things in the contemplation of beauty, as Abbot Suger had said about Chartres Cathedral in the Middle Ages. Beauty had nothing to do with morals. It could evidently inspire a passion to destroy as easily as a passion to love. I had been guilty of the kind of sentimentality which for three hundred years obscured the meaning of Nicolas Poussin's celebrated painting of shepherds taking their ease beside a tomb set in an idyllic pastoral landscape – on the tomb, the inscription *Et In Arcadia Ego*. Not until after the Second World War was it understood what Poussin had intended all along – that it was Death who speaks the words; Death visits Arcadia too.

*   *   *

I wasn't sure, any longer, who or what I could trust. Standing in the yard at Topside I had vowed to restore an overgrown garden of Eden out of a compost of memories. Now I was discovering that the garden had been teeming with weeds and predators from the first day. In Vladimir Nabokov's autobiography, *Speak, Memory*, Nabokov lauds 'the supreme achievement of memory, which is the masterly use it makes of innate harmonies when gathering to its fold the suspended and wandering tonalities of the past'. You may be sure that Nabokov protected those innate harmonies from anything approaching objective reality, for fear he'd have to cope with some uncomfortable discords.

There was every reason to suppose that, in the degree to which my recall of 1976 had played tricks on me, others of my memories had been selectively rose-tinted also. I thought about the 1960s and the way in which C. had bragged to Hélène about his place in history. What was the truth?

At the turn of the decade, in the summer of 1970, I went down by train and ferry to the Isle of Wight.

Thousands of my contemporaries made the same journey, in their T-shirts and Mao jackets, because this was to be the greatest pop festival since Woodstock, with Jimi Hendrix and Joan Baez and – the reason I was there – The Doors, with Jim Morrison chanting *Break on through to the other side!* The stage was at one end of a huge meadow which sloped upwards on one side towards the sea cliff. After an hour spent looking vainly for friends I'd lost in the crowd, I found a vantage-point, dumped my sleeping-bag on the ground, and sat down to listen to the sets.

Bearded or beaded figures in antique military tunics came round selling tobacco and Ritzo cigarette-papers to go with the hashish wrapped in Oxo-cube foil in the pockets of our donkey-jackets. As night fell, hundreds of candles were lit. One group after another pounded into the gathering darkness: until at last The Doors came on – John Densmore on drums, Robby Krieger on guitar, Ray Manzarek on bass and Jim Morrison singing *Come on baby light my fire!* – and the vast audience cheered and sang and exulted over them, punching their fists in the fragrant, smoky air.

That's the legend. That's what I would have told Hélène. As it happens, my one vivid image of the Isle of Wight pop festival is of waking up at 5.30 in the morning and stumbling to my feet. In the wintry light of dawn, a silver sea mist creeping in over the Tennyson Downs, bodies lay scattered and motionless as far as the eye could see, down as far as the Portakabins at the foot of the meadow. And on the distant stage, across the battlefield, the music had never stopped: I saw the tiny figure of Melanie singing in a reedy alto to the unconscious multitude. *What have they done to my song, Ma?*

And The Doors . . . was it really them I'd heard the night before? I can't remember now. Honestly I can't remember: perhaps it was the lysergic acid in the water supply. But the myth says they were there; just as the myth says Woodstock happened at Woodstock, when in reality the pop festival took place fifty miles away in an unromantic hamlet called Bethel, same name as the place where Amos prophesied woe to them that are at ease in Zion.

In those days it was still possible to be a fun-revolutionary and to regard logic as a cultural imposition to be discarded. As Tom Stoppard has his narrator say at the end of his 1974 play *Travesties* – 'I learned three things in Zurich during the war. I wrote them down. Firstly, you're either a revolutionary or you're not, and if you're not you might as well be an artist as anything else. Secondly, if you can't be an artist, you might as well be a revolutionary . . . I forget the third thing.'

In the end the nearest any of us came to revolution was a different kind of haircut, a different width of trouser, with each change of style making more headlines than the invasion of Antigua. It was possible, of course it was, to see each development as a new beginning, 'subverting the established categories' as we liked to think. Mobiles, collage novels, concrete poetry, happenings, the Dialectics of Liberation Conference at the Round House (its subject 'repressive tolerance') – they were all new beginnings, it's just that they didn't get to have a middle or an end.

The reason, I suppose, is that we had taken on the world before we had dealt with ourselves. As Daniel Cohn-Bendit said – talking at the LSE about the May 1968 *événements* in Paris, in which he was a leading figure – 'Our actions had outrun our theory and we were caught up in a vicious circle, constantly tempted out into the streets without time to think what to do.' The children had broken out of the nursery into the drawing-room, and they brought their toys with them, but when the toys broke they threw them away.

But by 1976, in Britain as in the United States, there was no more money for toys. The lustre had worn off the counter-culture; whatever real talents it nurtured had by then quietly moved into the mainstream. Drugs and the search for sensual gratification became more serious, more extreme. Timothy Leary's book *The Politics of Ecstasy* taught that the object of sex/LSD sessions was 'to make love with God'. The problem, as Leary himself discovered, was that the high you get the first time lessens in purity and intensity on each subsequent occasion. You don't reach heaven more than once; you fall further each time you reapply. But for people like this (and there turned out to have been plenty of them around Santa Cruz in 1976, romantics beached by the failure of their dreams) the satisfaction of the desire is never the death of the desire. They go on, and on, and on, until they kill the thing they love.

Beauty was *not* truth. While C. had been prancing through his summer in Spring Street, his companions had been struggling with enmities and anxieties, griefs and despairs, that were hidden from him. And now the rose-tinted spectacles were gone, I found that I was listening to a small insistent voice telling me that it hadn't wound up as such a glorious time, even for C.

*   *   *

Highway 17 into Santa Cruz through the mountains was still closed because of landslips after the earthquake. I had to cut down on to the coastal road back at Half Moon Bay to enter the town. I'd heard stories that there had been widespread devastation in Santa Cruz because so much of it was built on alluvial soil: but the outskirts showed nothing to suggest that I was entering a disaster zone. Mission Street in the sunshine looked unshocked and somnolent. The talk at the gas station and the drug store was all about the morning's visit by President Bush, although it was only twenty-four hours since the last body, of Robin Lynn Ortiz, had been dug out of the rubble of a coffee-shop she ran on Pacific Gardens Mall and carried away under the gaze of television cameras ('She will be remembered as a lover, an activist and a lesbian,' her grieving friend told the waiting microphones).

Even the old Victorian heart of Santa Cruz, between Front and Chestnut Streets, seemed perfectly normal at first glance, although quiet and empty, with several streets cordoned off from traffic. I was waved through a cordon to reach the makeshift Salvation Army depot at the rear of the City Hall. Trucks were unloading food and drink. Piles of clothes and toys, some of them brand-new, spilled out of the back of the building and lay heaped in the car park. I added Andrea's donation and parked nearby, outside the Santa Cruz Library where I had arranged to pick up some cuttings. I was beginning to see things I hadn't noticed before: the tell-tale cracks running up beside porches and under dormer windows, and skewing the wooden filigree ornamentation in vogue among the fashionable San Francisco types who summered here in the 1900s. Many of these fine old Victorian clapboarded houses, with their gables and turrets, had stood here for a hundred years or more. Now they looked like stroke victims, inwardly crumpled and tired.

At the end of the street where I stood was a haze of dust. Under it, cordoned off by firemen and police, was what remained of Pacific Gardens Mall, the commercial hub of downtown Santa Cruz. Dogs and their handlers were still sweeping the rubble of bricks and timbers for signs of life. I didn't intend to go and look any closer; I'd seen enough to know that the damage was worse than anything I'd witnessed in the Marina district of San Francisco. I thought of the places I'd revisited a few months ago – the bookshop-café, the Szechuan restaurant, the Del-Mar cinema, and the stately bulk of the Romanesque-style Cooper House, the old county courthouse building where we used to sit in the courtyard eating icecreams and listening to music. It, too, I later discovered, was condemned and knocked down.

I had Jan Furniss to check out at UCSC. On the way, I stopped off for lunch and took out the cuttings I'd xeroxed. I had expected a whole lot of stuff about the neuro-linguistic programme which Maria's friends had been working on. Instead there were pages and pages from the *Santa Cruz Sentinel* about a murder.

It happened in 1986. A thirty-one-year-old woman was shot dead in a rented town-house, and someone called Richard Bandler was indicted on suspicion of murdering her. His accuser, James Marino, once Bandler's closest friend, was the only person to witness the killing. He claimed that Bandler had been cocaine-dealing to save his behavioural programming enterprise from bankruptcy. The gun belonged to Bandler, and the Chief Deputy Sheriff of Santa Cruz claimed that there was 'biological and physiological evidence' to link Bandler to the shooting.

However, Marino had a police record for drug abuse

and theft. He failed to show up for pre-trial proceedings, and when he did take the witness stand he showed himself to be rambling and paranoid under questioning. A one-time patient of the psychotherapist, he testified that he and Bandler could heal the sick by placing hands on them. Various witnesses claimed that either Bandler or Marino had confessed to the murder. In the end everything turned upon the forensic evidence relating to the blood on Bandler's jeans and T-shirt . . . and the experts disagreed. In January 1988, Richard Bandler was acquitted.

I was looking at the findings of a National Research Council committee, which had concluded that there was no scientific evidence to support the claims of Neuro-Linguistic Programming, when one of the librarians came up. It intrigued her that this Englishman should have come all the way from London to study clippings on homicide cases. Santa Cruz, she told me proudly, was once known as the serial murder capital of the United States. Which period was I interested in?

'The mid-seventies.'

'I think there were some murders up in the Henry Cowell Park round about that time, 1976, I think. Let me go and have a look for you.'

The Henry Cowell Redwoods State Park, across the hillside from the University . . . in the whole of Santa Cruz there was nowhere more beautiful, or more precious in my memory. And yet it was true, what she said. She brought me the cuttings to prove it.

Two women, Vicky Bezore, aged thirty-one, and Mary Gorman, twenty-one, were driven that summer up Highway 9. Richard Anthony Sommerhalder, a twenty-nine-year-old shopkeeper who worked round the corner from his two victims in Rio del Mar, gave them a lift to a party. Towards the north-west corner of the Henry Cowell Redwoods Park, Sommerhalder somehow overpowered the women and dragged them into a thickly wooded area of hillside. There he stripped them naked, he stabbed them, and then he killed them by beating their heads against a rock. The bodies of Vicky Bezore and Mary Gorman lay undiscovered for seven weeks, decomposing on the hillside, while across the other side of the road, sometime during that period, Laura and I spent our last night together under the redwoods, in the place called the Garden of Eden by the San Lorenzo River.

(In July 1977 Richard Sommerhalder was sentenced to two consecutive five-year-to-life terms in prison. Superior Court Judge Harry Brauer, calling the slayings 'sophisticated and professional', urged that he 'be kept in prison for as long as it is legally possible to keep him there'. In January 1986, after eight years in prison, Sommerhalder was paroled. Shortly afterwards he was found bleeding by police after punching his fist through a window during an argument. Two months later he was back inside, after threatening the life of his parole officer. But by January 1988, according to the *Santa Cruz Sentinel*, he had been set free into the community again and was currently living in a trailer park in Aptos.)

I left the library and drove up the hill. The teasing memory which, more than any other, had sent me on this quest for a vanished summer had been of the three naked girls playing with the gopher snake which crawled out of the scrub as we planted squash in Howard's vegetable garden under the warm sun. Now, with a vividness which almost sent me off the road, the snake metamorphosed into a rattlesnake and the girls' laughter into screams, and I stood there paralysed, unable to move or cry out.

I thought of something Hélène had told me in Halifax. On campus, in the summer of 1976, she had gone up with a group of other people behind Merrill College to a clearing in the redwoods. There, naked or topless, they had talked and studied their books, and gradually drifted back. Hélène went on reading. Hearing a noise she looked up and realized that she was all alone, and saw a man's face staring at her through the bushes. She screamed and got up; grabbing her top, she began running. The man came after her. Hélène screamed again and heard a shout from the direction of Merrill. The man stopped chasing her and vanished into the woods.

In Santa Cruz I turned right on Highland and drove up Spring Street. Nothing up here seemed to be affected by the earthquake. The Messiah Lutheran Church and the University Baptist Church on the corner still stood neat and wooden-gabled like buildings in a German fairytale. Further up, on what I saw now was really rather an unremarkable street, came the little brick or white-painted bungalows with their mailboxes and trim front gardens and compacts in the driveway. At the top, where my green hill-meadows began, a new wire fence had been erected, replacing the old hedgerow.

Behind it, mounted in a ten-foot-high redwood surround which had been freshly dug in beside where the old Felton wagon-road came down, stood a big metal sign.

I studied this sign for a while. Welcome to Pogonip. Looking around, I saw that a couple of new telephone poles

Christopher Hudson

POGONIP

The City of Santa Cruz welcomes you.
Visitors are responsible to know and follow
these regulations.

<u>Hours of Operation</u>

| Summer | Apr. 1 to Oct. 31 | Sunrise–7pm |
| Winter | Nov. 1 to Mar. 31 | Sunrise–4pm |

<u>The Following Activities Are Prohibited ...</u>

Camping	Firearms	Hunting
Alcohol	Smoking	Archery
Horses	Fires	Littering
Bicycles	Bathing	Fireworks
Wood collecting	Motor vehicles	Flora collecting

<u>Hikers/Walkers Must Stay On Trails</u>

<u>For Your Own Safety Do Not Touch Or Feed Livestock</u>
<u>All Dogs Must Be Kept On Leash</u>

The Pogonip Club and Road are Private. No public access.

had been put in; perhaps there were going to be telephone points along between the arroyos where hikers could call up and get a recorded message about the scenic view. With a heavy heart I walked up the drive.

Topside was still there. It had not been destroyed by the earthquake. It looked fine, to me. I rang the bell and asked the wispy-bearded student who came to the door if the house had suffered damage.

He looked at me suspiciously. When I explained that I wasn't a city official, that I'd lived in the house a long time ago, he relaxed and nodded. There had been some damage. A lot of stuff had fallen off the walls and shelves. A water-main had burst; they were still clearing up after it. And the chimney, the white chimney in the middle of the house which came out just below the ridge tiles, had shifted half an inch in the first big shake. It would have to come down and be rebuilt.

That would be costly. I wondered what the three Paginhart children who now jointly owned the house would do. Howard Tellier had told me that they didn't always get along so well, but they might easily end up agreeing to sell the place. They could make such a good profit.

I'd mentioned this to Rick, who'd been interested. Since I'd been to see him in Detroit and we'd talked about the book I was writing, he'd come back out to the West Coast and made a special journey to revisit Spring Street. When I'd spoken to him on the phone he reckoned that Topside would have doubled or trebled in value since the late 1970s. It would be worth at least a million dollars – more than a million if the plot could be sub-divided and some developer ran a road past the house. There were already eight or ten big luxury homes where the old ranch had been, and more lots could be gouged out of the undergrowth. Spring Street Estate! – though Rick thought that land-use controls in Santa Cruz nowadays would probably be too strict to permit that. There was a wistful note in his voice. Rick would have liked to have the money to buy Topside himself.

I drove on to UCSC. The campus was closed, I was told, and wasn't due to open for a day or two. Although the earthquake had caused no major damage it had badly shocked many of the students. And up here, so close to the epicentre, the aftershocks were still occurring at frequent intervals.

Laura and her husband Jim had invited me to have supper with them in Aptos and stay the night. I had time to spare, and called in for a drink with one of UCSC's longest-serving and most distinguished professors, whom I hadn't seen for thirteen years. I wanted to know what had happened to UCSC since 1976. Was it still a beacon on a hill, serving as a model for the best kind of higher education? How had the college system held up at Santa Cruz? Was Arcadia still working?

My old acquaintance took his time before answering. He poured two stiff whiskies with deliberation, and raised his glass.

'To the heroic age of UCSC!' he proclaimed. 'It started in the early seventies and lasted for about five years – and you must have seen the end of it!'

Things had changed since Clark Kerr identified the three major administrative problems on a campus as sex for the students, athletics for the alumni and parking for the faculty. It turned out that, in the late 1970s and early 1980s, the University of California, Santa Cruz, had pitched into a dramatic decline. The standard of admissions slumped. It still wasn't back to what it had been. UCSC had fallen prey to the commercialization it had struggled so valiantly to avoid. It had turned into a run-of-the-mill State university organized along traditional departmental lines, with an emphasis on specialization and business-oriented studies.

The University of Arcadia had not caved in to outside pressures. The failure had come from within. To make its utopian programme work, each college needed faculty to cover the whole range of curricular subjects – and soon enough this proved impossible to sustain. A physicist didn't want to operate from an arts college; a medievalist didn't feel at home in a science college. Autonomous departments began to emerge and challenge the authority of the colleges. UCSC faculty, fearful of the power which could be exercised by these Boards of Studies, all wanted a piece of the cake. Gradually the committees expanded, took on more powers including the development of graduate programmes, and became vulnerable to all those pressures which the founders of UCSC had set out deliberately to avoid.

The campus became a battleground. The colleges accused the boards of selling out to specialized professional interests. The boards accused the colleges of wasting faculty and student time with irrelevant, mickey-mouse courses. Undergraduates were neglected as faculty fought their private battles. There were bitter recriminations over promotion and hiring, with the colleges wanting to promote people internally on merit and the boards wanting to stick to the traditional, constricting formula of defining the worth of teachers by what they'd had published in books and specialized journals. The utopian vision of Clark Kerr and Dean

McHenry dissipated in an atmosphere of rancour and distrust.

In the end, self-interest predominated; a succession of Chancellors found themselves unable to sustain the integrity of the college ideal. And perhaps it never was much more than a pipe-dream. The generation of undergraduates who started applying to universities in the mid-1970s, in the States as in Britain, were impatient with grand theories of a liberal education. The job market was shrinking; they wanted qualifications which would buy them a ticket on the gravy train. In any case the American (and British) business community had no preference for quizzical, sceptical, highly educated graduates. They wanted, and still want, specialized talents and narrow-focused minds.

And who's to say that they are wrong? Liberal education taken to its logical extreme breeds utopian ideals. Eventually a new Chancellor arrived who saw the writing on the wall. He stripped the colleges of their academic role and gave it to the Boards of Studies. Most interdisciplinary courses disappeared. UCSC, which at the time C. was there used to offer a course on Love, was now negotiating for permission to build a huge industrial park on campus for sponsored high-tech research.

My professor saw signs that things were improving. Admissions were picking up again. UCSC planned to expand from 8,000 students to 20,000 students during this decade. But he didn't enjoy living here any more. The University had changed for the worse, and so had Santa Cruz itself. It used to be (as Rick once described it to me) basically a resort town with a counter-culture built in on one side and a university on the other, and the self-sufficient people trying to build their lives in between. Now its population had more than doubled in the past twenty years, its roads were jammed, its tranquil atmosphere destroyed. The professor himself was leaving, as he told me, and moving to Berkeley.

It was, I was coming to realize, as pointless to devise ideal blueprints for the future as it was to imagine golden ages in the past. Howard hadn't been the first to discover that. Frank E. Manuel, Kenan Professor of History at New York University, spent twenty-five years working in collaboration with his wife Fritzie on an exhaustive study of *Utopian Thought in the Western World*, and they came to the conclusion that most utopian thinkers were emotional cripples, sublimating their longing to return to the paradise of the womb in fantasies of wish-fulfilment. Thomas More suffered from 'controlled rage'. Francis Bacon had a 'classically anal personality'. Bakunin was 'riddled with anxiety over his impotence'.

Myths of Arcadia hark back, as I've said, to Virgil's pastoral poems with their shepherds and shepherdesses, picturesque landscapes and music as the food of love. But if you look closely, you'll see that Virgil sets only one of his *Eclogues* in Arcadia. The bucolic poems have much more ominous overtones, as his shepherds recognize that poetry is powerless in a world controlled by conquest and competition for land. And Arcadia itself, even in Virgil's day, was already a literary conceit.

On the way over to Aptos I stopped and got out of the car, and sat on the cliff, at a point where the ocean scoops a shallow curve out of the great crescent of Monterey Bay. The breakers were disappointing; a few surfers were up but

the rest trod water idly, waiting for something bigger to
happen by. C. had come out here with Laura in July, thirteen
years ago, and watched boys ride the waves, balancing and
zig-zagging, until there was nothing to carry them forward
and they sank. Inland, the leaves were dark and the ground
was dusty. The summer had been hot and increasingly dry.
Santa Cruz had declared a water shortage.

All this time C. had put off making a decision about his
life because it was likely to be irrevocable, and the very idea
of permanence struck him as an obscenity. In this paradise
of his, words like 'commitment' or even 'choice' were too
cruelly determinist to contemplate. There were no absolutes,
no divine prohibitions; only (as Susan Sontag called it) the
obliteration of the personality in the pursuit of happiness.
Except that he was beginning to ask himself if this really
was happiness. He lay in the orchard under the orange trees
thinking his green thoughts in a green shade, and when he
roused himself and went up to campus, or into town, or
drove up to San Francisco to see friends and have his British
passport renewed (his black eye visible to this day in the
passport photograph) it was as if his feet were three inches
off the ground. Enjoyment came so easily that there was no
pleasure left in surrendering to it.

His Harkness Fellowship had eleven months to run. It
was one of the terms of the award that Fellows should
return home after their period of study expired. C. had no
desire to become an academic. The scholastic impulse which
had taken him to Chicago was fading in the Californian
sun. He loved Laura; he was nevertheless becoming
conscious that his love for her was bound up with a
particular place and time which seemed to have no reference
to the outside world. Meanwhile his girlfriend in England

was sending him letters, full of love and longing, which in their every detail connected him to a world that was intimate to him, of names and addresses, parents and friends, money and books and careers.

Laura was talking to him about the invitation she had to teach summer school in Berkeley. The problem was, Robert would be in Berkeley. She didn't have to go: she had all the books she needed for her thesis research on Ariosto and Renaissance poetry right here in Santa Cruz.

C. had read some of Ariosto's great epic, *Orlando Furioso*. There is an earthly paradise in it, rather traditionally presented, where Astolfo meets St John and the prophets; but there is also a far more beautiful paradise Ariosto describes, the garden of Alcina. Only gradually do you begin to realize that everything is not what it seems. The garden of Alcina reflects back the desires and illusions of those who wander in it. It sets no conditions. Its danger lies not in what it does to you but in what it allows you to do to yourself.

'I can't decide for you,' C. said to Laura then. 'I think you should do what you think is right for you.'

'Do what I think is *right?*'

She looked at him, with a kind of bewildered despair. She and he had detached themselves from that intimacy with the natural world which accompanies the experience of romantic and sentimental love: and, once outside that enchanted circle, the innocence of the New World had come up against the ambiguity of the Old. C. had been one of the few people she had ever known who could share her pure vision of the world, and suddenly it was as if he had closed his eyes and turned his head.

At the end of East Cliff Drive, out Soquel way, the ocean

road becomes plain Cliff Drive. It was here, in a house on the cliffs overshadowed by a huge tree, that one of their friends from HistCon threw a party to celebrate the end of the semester. C. contacted Laura, to arrange where to pick her up.

'Why don't you come with us?' she said.

'Who's us?'

'With Robert and me.'

'Oh.'

'Or you can take your car and we'll meet you there.'

Which is what C. did. In the event they arrived together – a weird sight, as somebody told me thirteen years later, the weirdest thing he'd seen all summer, Laura on the arm of her two lovers, one of them still bruised by a punch thrown by his rival. The living-room had doors out onto the lawn; lights were strung around the place and there was plenty to drink. Tammy Wynette was belting out 'Stand by Your Man'. C.'s New York friends were over by the window with Mike, Laura's tutor who had an apartment on Rincon Street. C. went over to talk to them. When he looked round, Laura had disappeared. He saw her dancing with Robert, and went to get a drink.

Several drinks later and it was Diana Ross singing 'Do You Know Where You're Going To?'. Couples moved dreamily round the floor. C. looked for Laura and couldn't see her. He went out into the cliff-top garden. Somewhere below the sea groaned and fell back on the invisible rocks. In the shadowy light he could see all the familiar pairs he had come to know during the course of the summer, people who had been together all along or who had separated and come together again. He heard a familiar voice, lilting with amusement, expostulation, and saw Laura and Robert walking hand in hand, across the grass, away from the house, out of the circle of light.

C. got into his car and drove back to Spring Street. He knew that he couldn't pretend any longer; the gates were closing. Laura was insisting that he make his mind up. It was now or never, England or California; old world or new. Either he broke off relations with all that was precious to him at home and stayed on with Laura, or else it was over between the two of them.

Choice. Commitment. C. couldn't handle it. He had reached a point of equilibrium at which all his systems rebelled against the act of decision. He lay on his bed in the alcove, in the dark, and broke into sobs of confusion and self-pity. He had come all this way seeking wisdom and self-knowledge, only to discover that he didn't really know himself at all.

At four in the morning, choking with tears, C. made a phone call to England. Ten days later he drove to San Francisco and collected his girlfriend from the airport, and began the process of awakening from a dream. He moved out of Spring Street, since his alcove was much too small for both of them, and rented Mike's comfortable apartment on Rincon. They lived there for five weeks, spending a lot of time in bed, or buying groceries or watching cable TV. At this time, because C. felt the need to get back to writing about Paradise, he contacted the University of Virginia, Charlottesville, and arranged to spend the remainder of his Fellowship there, starting in the autumn. He had learned this much: that he could only write about Paradise from the perspective of the Fall.

But it was a gentle awakening. For one thing, the dream still lay around him, its light, its colour, its sights and sounds and smells. Driving back up Spring Street, as C. occasionally did, and turning down the narrow drive to his lost Eden, no angel with a flaming sword barred his way in. Howard shook his hand. Hélène threw her arms round his neck. Rafiki brushed his leg as she stalked past from Andrea's rooms. In the vegetable garden the string beans were shooting up. Soon the squash would be ready. If he looked upon these things differently, the change was all within him. In coming to terms with his future, C. had fallen under the rules of time.

*   *   *

That end-of-semester party in Cliff Drive, when she had walked out of the circle of light, was not the last C. was to see of Laura. In the brief time he had left, after his girlfriend had gone back to London, he would drive up to Berkeley, where Laura was teaching summer school, and they would play tennis together in the Rosegarden, on the shale courts that jut out on stilts above the slope of the hill.

She was happy to see him, and especially happy to be away from Robert, who had spent most of the last few weeks in Soquel working at his doctoral thesis. Now that C. was back in the real world again, the tensions which had grown up between him and Laura seemed to fall away. His love for her was still strong, but much more selfish now. The die was cast. He knew that in a few weeks he would be leaving California. He also was pretty sure that he would not be coming back. At some stage soon he would open a door and step through into his other life, my life, which was set up for him. Laura had no doors to open, no other life to step into.

In early September C. set aside his love story, unfinished. In the Rincon apartment he gave a couple of farewell dinners and started packing his bags. Howard Tellier's parting gift was two brown capsules of MDA, the derivative of the Mexican peyote drug mescaline. The day before C. left Santa Cruz, he and Laura took the MDA and set out for the Garden of Eden.

According to the official guide, the Garden of Eden was situated in the Henry Cowell Redwoods State Park, at the end of the Ox Road Trail. In the early evening they drove round the north side of the hill on which the University stood and up Highway 9 to a roadside pullout at the edge of the park. There were still a few hikers and sightseers around: but as C. and Laura cast about to find the trail, and walked deeper into the redwood forest, the sound of other voices died away. Soon the noise of cars on the highway was swallowed up too. Carrying a blanket and water bottles they followed the trail, keeping to their left the sound of running water. After a while there was a stream to cross, and a sloping wall of fern-covered rock. They climbed it, and arrived at a stretch of broad shallow-banked water shining in the evening sun.

It was a place where the San Lorenzo River, dropping lazily from the Santa Cruz mountains, curved round a sandy spur and opened up into a wide pool before continuing its journey to the sea. All around grew stands of redwood, madrone and tanbark oak, enclosing the river-pool in cliffs of evergreen. The only sound to be heard was the gentle splash of the stream running down the bank into the calm water. Treading softly, afraid to break the silence, Laura and C. stepped down between the rocks and spread the blanket on the sand.

That night they had the park to themselves, and it participated in their hallucination. It patterned itself to the curves of their bodies in the sand. It turned them into living rainbows of iridescence when they went swimming in the last of the sun. When the day died into night and was buried everywhere in shadows, it transformed the giant trees above their heads into guardian spirits ministering to their tranquillity. As never before or since, the universe revealed itself, tenderly and intimately, as a living presence watching over them and participating in every motion of their heads and hands. The moon rose and set for them. The stars moved knowingly in the heavens. Brush of wind in the branches, plucking of water, stirring of undergrowth combined in a murmurous conversation which Laura seemed to be having with him and he with Laura, all the night through.

Howard, they decided, was not a chemist so much as an alchemist who had discovered the philosopher's stone whereby all ideas were subsumed into one all-encompassing idea – though what that was they couldn't, for the moment, be quite sure. But whatever it might be, it certainly encompassed the two of them as they lay there talking familiarly of time and space. They were part of the idea, the idea of themselves, as something that could not ever be refuted.

About an hour after nightfall they saw the flicker of a park warden's torch through the trees. Then, around midnight, they heard the delicate footsteps of a deer as it picked its way over the stones and came down to the pool to drink. In the first light of dawn they bequeathed the hazy imprint of themselves to the sand by the river, and set off through the forest back to the car. In C.'s Rincon apartment they showered and slept, still in a dream of Eden. Then they hugged each other, in the desolate morning, and C. got into the car and drove away to the other side of America.

It was Labor Day weekend, but there wasn't much traffic going east across the San Joaquin Valley. Not many hitchhikers either, although C. was looking out for company to stop his mind seizing on thoughts of absence and loss. He knew that during the night with Laura under the redwoods he had experienced something unforgettable, and that she was somehow responsible for it: she had conspired with the beauty and sanctity of the place to cast an enchantment over him which he should not be able to throw off. He was driving further and further away, and yet it was Laura's face he kept seeing, Laura's voice he kept hearing, every time he stopped for food or gas, or crossed a motel forecourt, or pulled in at a street corner to get a can of Coke.

He couldn't rid himself of the grief he felt. The further away from Eden he drove, into the wilderness of the world, the worse it became. And C. had inflicted this expulsion on himself. Nobody had forced him to leave. Apollo had vanquished Dionysus; culture had won out over instinct. *Footfalls echo in the memory Down the passage which we did not take* . . . he had walked down that passage; he had opened that door, into the rose-garden. Only to discover that it wasn't the door into his future, but just another version of his past.

He drove up into Yosemite Valley and grieved at its empty magnificence. Last night he had heard, he had communicated; now he listened in vain. He went up into the high Sierras. They were barren of snow, barren of meaning, barren of majesty. Descending, on the far side, into wasteland, he drove on through the gathering darkness. At Lone Pine he turned off east through the sagebrush and parched brown earth towards Death Valley.

By now it was midnight, past midnight, and as C. drove down five thousand feet from the Panamint pass to the valley floor it grew hotter and hotter until he could hardly breathe. The headlights picked out a sign at the side of the desert road. He was below sea level, passing through the Devil's Cornfield. Too tired to drive any further, he stopped off in a lay-by, disturbing a coyote which slunk away in the dark. Here was where he deserved to be: in the abyss, in the darkness, alone. He got out his sleeping-bag and laid it on the ground and, woken at intervals by insects crawling across his face and neck, he slept the sleep of the damned.

But who, any longer, are the damned or saved? Today, Paradise is nothing but a joke, a travesty, an arid emblem of itself, scarcely more than a travel-brochure synonym for happiness. This was the conclusion C. reached in Charlottesville, Virginia, during the final period of his Fellowship.

The reality of an earthly paradise, which was already fading in Europe by the time the young Alexander Pope made a pretty couplet of it in 1713 –

> *The Groves of Eden, vanished now so long,*
> *Live in description, and look green in song*

– survived for another hundred years and more in America.

Milton's vision of Eden crossed the Atlantic with his Puritan contemporaries in the *Mayflower*. The Puritan historians of New England thought explicitly in terms of a redemptive mission. At the beginning of the eighteenth century Cotton Mather proclaimed that the lost Eden had been replanted by God in the Garden of America. The providential note is echoed in the Constitution of the United States and – *Novus ordo saeclorum* – on every dollar bill in circulation.

Three thousand miles of ocean separated the settlers from the tired disbelief of the Old World. Up at least until the middle of the nineteenth century the idea of America as a second Eden held sway, as the early pioneers made their way through a landscape such as no man will ever see again – the last unspoiled wilderness of the temperate zone. *In the beginning all the world was America*, wrote John Locke three hundred years ago. In the paintings of Albert Bierstadt or Thomas Doughty, landscape is a religious experience, speaking of a time before the Fall. But gradually, as railways, farms and factories followed the settlers westwards across the continent, the first notes of disillusion could be heard.

On the morning of 27 July 1844, Nathaniel Hawthorne's meditations in the paradisal setting of Sleepy Hollow near Concord, Massachusetts, were suddenly disturbed by the shriek and whistle of a locomotive, which 'brings the noisy world into the midst of our slumbrous peace'. It is a famous episode which – like the big steamboat in Mark Twain's *Huckleberry Finn* which storms out of the night like a black cloud and smashes through the raft on which Huck and Jim are peacefully floating down the Mississippi – is regularly used to illustrate the crumbling of the pastoral ideal under the hammer-blows of the machine age. In the writings of Hawthorne, Melville and Twain, the Edenic theme is seen to have another side to it: innocence lost, opportunities squandered, and Adam given no third chance.

And then came Darwin. *The Origin of Species* and the book of Genesis could not both be literally true. To this day creationists continue to struggle against Darwin's proofs of natural selection. A survey in 1980 indicated that almost half the adult population of the United States believed itself to be directly descended from Adam and Eve. Even as C. was driving eastwards, high schools in Dallas, Texas, were voting to use a new textbook in their biology classes. Called *A Search for Order in Complexity*, it proposed that God created Adam out of the dust of the ground, and took one of his ribs while he slept and made out of it Eve his wife. Then it appended Darwin's theory of evolution and invited students to choose their preference.

But the damage was done, a hundred years before. Marx commented that Darwinism was the ethos of capitalism projected on to nature: and it was true that the theory of the survival of the fittest gave a licence to materialism and greed unconstrained by Christian ethics. The end of paradise, the emptiness of the skies, spurred men on to create heavens on earth, no matter what the cost. If man was no longer made in God's image, he could do his best to make himself a god. From Andrew Carnegie to Donald Trump, social Darwinism has flourished in opposition to morality.

Other ethical systems have attempted to replace the exploded philosophy of Milton's God. In 1976 in California, New Ageism was already a force to be reckoned with. Bookshops in Santa Cruz offered whole sections devoted to holistic thinking – the occult, alternative medicine, Eastern religions, organic muesli, nature and natural forces. The phrase 'green revolution' came into currency at the 1970 Stockholm Conference on the Environment, which first alerted public opinion to the consequences of pollution of the biosphere. The ecological movements it generated spawned quasi-religious offshoots – the worship of the living planet, Gaia; the back-to-nature religiosity of the radical ecologists. The New Ageists have taken these on board too.

All these manifestations of heightened consciousness, these attempts to 'listen to the truth in one's own being', in C.'s view represented a domestication of the sacred. There was no disciplined framework of meaning to it, none of the fire and ice of God. As G. K. Chesterton wisely remarked, when people stop believing in God they don't then believe in nothing, they believe in everything. Good and evil become value-judgements. Morality is relative. For the idea of progress is substituted the idea of change.

In the Christian world order, evil was the consequence of sin, and sin was the consequence of the Fall, the work of the Devil. Christians used to understand very well the purpose of Paradise, or Heaven, in their cosmology. It was the reward of good, as Hell was the reward of evil. In this formula, under the scrutiny of an omniscient but merciful God, resided the source and impulse of morality. By abolishing Heaven and Hell, twentieth-century secular culture destroyed the hope of redemption. It replaced religious optimism with a deep underlying pessimism which sees evil as dispersed through history and self-knowledge as the only consolation in the face of nothingness. It is the arid consolation which Proust experiences, walking in the Bois de Boulogne and finding it much changed from the old days when he used to encounter Mme Swann –

'And all these new elements in the spectacle destroyed the

Christopher Hudson

faith which had once given it consistency, unity, life, in my eyes. They passed before me in a disordered way, at random, without reality, having none of the intrinsic beauty which had once manifested itself to me in the scene as a whole . . . But when a faith vanishes, there survives it – and more and more passionately, to hide the loss of the ability we once possessed to impart reality to new things – a superstitious attachment to the old things we did have faith in, as if it was in them and not in us that deity resided, and as if our present lack of belief could be ascribed to a cause outside of ourselves: the death of the Gods.'

C. had nowhere left to go, it seemed to him, as, woken by the dawn, parched and sore, he climbed out of Death Valley, past the first scattering of tourists taking pictures at Zabriskie Point. He was at one with William Blake, for whom man's birth was itself the Fall, and whose illustrations read into Milton's poem the catastrophic victory of Reason over man's innate passion and desire.

Then, coming out of Las Vegas in the early afternoon, he picked up a Chicano bound for Tucson, Arizona. Short and dark and stocky, with a tough, scarred face and a badly broken nose, he was cradling a small kitten in his arms. He told C. her name was Shadow. He'd rescued her eighteen hours before in a Las Vegas alleyway from the jaws of a 'lady dog' which had killed the rest of the litter. Now he was taking her to his mother in Tucson, who was holding a cheque for him. His three daughters were there too, and the eldest needed new clothes. He'd been on the road three days, hitching from Newark, New Jersey, where there'd been work in a cannery. He showed me his hands, they were cracked and bruised. $395 a month, to put his girls through school.

One finger was swollen and bent. He told C. that he'd been a prizefighter most of his life, winning a slew of lightweight championships and having Frank Sinatra say 'Gimme five' and put a $100 bill into his boxing glove. Then came Vietnam.

The Chicano looked at C. His eyes were small and black and wild, but not unfriendly. He had a younger sister he called Tomboy ('She went with the men, didn't take her panties off to piss' – laughter) and when he went out with the Marines, Tomboy came too, out of love for him. She worked as a secretary in Saigon, typing for the Marines. 'She was killed. They kept it from me for thirty days. She was shot through the window by a sniper. I was mad. I wanted to kill everybody – kill! kill! kill! – do you understand, the death of someone you love?'

He stared at C. expressionlessly. His stint in Vietnam was supposed to be over, but he went back for another year. 'You know, if you want to die, I think it is very difficult?' One day he was releasing prisoners. They were across the river and started shooting. They got him in both legs, in the spine, in the face. He threw grenades back at them and got a Bronze Star for it, and still he wanted to go back. 'My sister, she was a little tomboy. Really, a tomboy.'

C. gave him a can of Coors. 'Look out the back,' the Chicano kept saying as he drank, holding the sleeping kitten in his other hand. He punched C. in the arm. 'You're a good guy,' he said. 'Know that? You're a good guy.' He drank. 'Keep looking,' he advised. 'Keep looking.'

C. put him out at Kingman and drove on. The temperature was in the high 90s; he kept wiping the sweat out of his eyes. Don't give up, *keep looking*. The heat stuck down all that day and all night. All next morning, too, as C. drove east towards New Mexico, with the thunderclouds massed to the north over the Colorado River. And then at last, somewhere north of Cameron, in the vivid glow of the Painted Desert, the weather broke. The rain came down in floods, cleaning the air, pounding against the windscreen. And he could see clear again.

*   *   *

Laura and Jim were renting a large modern detached house in an estate of large modern detached houses in a newly developed part of Rio del Mar, near the ocean. In the dark I lost my way. I tried Dolphin Drive and Seascape Boulevard, and made sorties along Via Novella, Via Trinita, Via Lantana and Via Medici before finding the address I was after. The bell that I rang sounded a twin chime. Laura came to the door and gave me a hug. She and Jim had eaten dinner already, but there was pizza in the oven and a glass of beer. I sat at the table along from the breakfast bar and made conversation about the earthquake.

Jim, a gentle, inquisitive man with an air of calm good humour, nodded gravely as I described the devastation in Santa Cruz. The kettle boiled. Laura got up to make some coffee. She was radiant with happiness: and there was one very visible reason for it. After giving up almost all hope of ever having a baby, Laura was pregnant. It had happened not long after she had left Los Angeles, an unexpected, almost miraculous conception which was now safely on the way. Laura had written a card to me in

London – 'Need I tell you how happy I am? I know you'll understand.'

When C. left California in September 1976 she had quitted her apartment in Soquel and gone to live in a trailer up in the hills, on North Branciforte, to get away from Robert. Not long afterwards Robert left Santa Cruz and flew to London, to carry on his research. For the next two years Laura lived by herself: first in the trailer and then in a carriage-house close by the sea on West Cliff Drive.

She told C. about it in her letters, sent to the Blue Mountains in Virginia where he had gone to live for the last nine months of his Fellowship. She had an attic room in a three-storey Victorian house, with a view over Monterey Bay to the right, and the early-morning mist rising off the San Lorenzo Valley. In the garden were redwoods, elms and palm trees, three silver olive trees, a Catalpa and a Norfolk Island pine. It was easier for her to describe what she was seeing than what she was thinking or feeling. This was the loneliest period of her life. She had always been on a wavelength that few other people could catch or attune to; now she felt as if she was sending messages out into the void.

After C. left Santa Cruz she came back to Howard for some more of his MDA, in the hope that it could take her back on the journey we had travelled together. Long hours she spent on her bed in the attic room staring up through the skylight at the clouds and stars. That was where she learned the names of the constellations she had pointed out to me in Los Angeles when we went back to her house for coffee.

Robert wrote to her from England and begged her to join him. He could not go on living without her. Laura was on the point of acquiescing in an affair with a married man which was in danger of destroying her professionally as well as emotionally. She had to get away . . . she arranged a research post in London and went to see Robert. At once, with nowhere to turn and no one to turn to, the old dependence reasserted itself. Eventually she found the strength to leave Robert a second time and fly back to the United States. Robert disappeared. He went home. The last news of him that reached her was that he had taken his doctoral thesis on the Classical revival, the product of ten or twelve years' hard labour, and thrown it on the fire.

We had come through, Laura and I, in our different ways. She looked more at peace with herself than I had ever seen her. Everything in their lives had changed for the better. Laura's doctorate had been finished and approved. So highly was it thought of, that offers of interviews for tenured university posts were already coming in. Jim had finished his political campaign work in Sacramento and could now be with her until the baby was born. Watching Laura, the way she glowed with delight to have Jim and me sitting at her table, I thought back to our meeting in Los Angeles. She had changed more in six months than in the previous six years. The anxiety had left her face. The nervousness was gone. She was a wife; she was about to become a mother. She was engaged in the process of drawing her family round her. She talked about their neighbours in Rio del Mar. She talked about taking up golf at the nearby Seascape Golf Course.

Perhaps I should have been dismayed. Instead I felt both happy for her and strangely relieved. In Los Angeles I had created a nexus of feelings around our shared memories which was too intense to sustain in the abstract. I had drawn Laura, perhaps against her better judgement, into a fire of nostalgia about a relationship which could never have been replicated, even if our circumstances had been different.

There were no aftershocks that night. In the morning, the three of us went walking along the cliffs, in the narrow strip of grassy land which had not yet been built over. I told them the extraordinary stories of Hélène and Andrea. We talked about the effects of memory, and the incuriousness which enabled some of the people I'd met to go on from year to year without thinking about their lives or analyzing the lessons of the past. Laura was teaching at Stanford; the University of California Press was prepared to publish her dissertation. But they were restless, ready to move on. California didn't hold the magic for them it once had had.

I said goodbye to Jim at the door of their new home. Laura came out to the car. I kissed her and drove away, back the short distance to Santa Cruz. On impulse, I stopped off at Rincon, to look at the row of redwood apartments where C. had spent the last part of that summer of 1976. Built on stilts against the steeply-rising hill, with garage space underneath, dwarfed by the high stand of eucalyptus which had brushed with silver leaves against the balcony at night making a sound like the sea, they looked exactly as I remembered them. I was contemplating going up to look at C.'s old apartment, when a man in sneakers and blue dungarees strolled up.

'Wait about,' he said. 'Don't go up there. Is that place yours?'

I explained what I was doing there. He nodded.

'It's condemned,' he declared.

He was a building surveyor. He pointed out to me cracks that I hadn't seen in the retaining brick walls. He showed me where one or two of the stilts were buckling, where a staircase had come away at the top.

'These are all condemned,' he said. 'Have a nice day now.'

The University was still closed. Jan Furniss would have to wait for another time. There was nothing more I could do; I was due to be in Los Angeles tomorrow to catch a flight back to London.

It didn't matter. I had found the missing person I'd gone looking for. I'd tracked him into the enchanted garden of Spring Street, that summer long ago, and shadowed his footsteps. I'd uncovered a man who, in common with so many of his 1960s generation, was motivated by a desperate unwillingness to let go of his youth. The reasons he had embarked upon a study of Paradise were more personal and complex than he was prepared to admit, even to himself. A desire to escape . . . but above all a desire to return, to build a bridge back to childhood and reassemble something which once was whole.

People are not always of the country in which they are born, wrote Théophile Gautier and, when you are prey to such a condition, you search everywhere for your true country. C. went searching for his true country and for a time he thought he had found it. The space and light and colours of the California hill-meadows returned to him a sense of Africa and his earliest childhood where, as Thomas Traherne describes it in his *Centuries of Meditations, Eternity was manifest in the Light of the Day, and something infinite behind everything appeared: which talked with my expectation and moved my desire.* The intimacy of his relationships in Spring Street – not only with Laura but with the household in Topside who took him into their lives with such warmth and openness – also returned him to a time before loneliness and alienation set in, as an only child sent thousands of miles away to a chill schoolyard and a stern church.

Perhaps it was the lack of some feeling of blessing inside him which led him to seek his blessings in external things, and find them in such profusion that summer. But he wouldn't let go. He became the child he was remembering. His study of Paradise finished up rejecting the Christian element almost completely and focusing on the infantile narcissism of the mystic. In doing so he neglected his original aim, which was to demonstrate how the Paradise theme engages the artistic imagination at its most exalted.

C. had journeyed out to America hoping to recover a sense of faith – at any rate in himself – through the exercise of reason. Under the influence of Spring Street, and Laura, reason had fallen away, and he'd succumbed to the temptation of taking paradise at face value – only to sink into despair when it turned out to be illusory, as fundamentally unserious as the University of Arcadia itself. This man who had come away from England believing that self-knowledge was the ultimate touchstone of the truth of things had ended up evading the truth at every turn.

But what am I doing, saying this? Look, look in the mirror. I can't any longer deny it – I had gone back, thirteen years later, on the same quest – to recapture time and make it stand still. And now, at last, I know the reason he went missing, the Englishman in Spring Street: it's that he spelled the end of my youth, when he left Laura and the false paradise and drove away into the wilderness of the real world.

I shan't go back. I've taken a long look at my youth, and it isn't the golden country I once imagined. Talking to Howard and the others I was reminded of the saving grace of his country, which is to believe that the golden age was not lost in the past but is still attainable . . . *God gave man a second chance in America.* I was fortunate enough to find my girlfriend waiting for me when I got to England, and to discover that lasting love isn't something you build in gardens of Eden but in the wilderness beyond, with hard work and disappointments commingled with the marvellous things. Unchanging delight is as meaningless a notion as Heaven without Hell; happiness depends on contrast, and change. Experience of good and evil if you like: and with that knowledge may come wisdom, truth, maturity – all the qualities which Adam lacked in Paradise.

The next morning, I started up Route 9 towards Los Angeles, going the long way round to Highway 101 through the Santa Cruz mountains. Within four miles I was stopped by barriers and police cars across the road. Nothing could get through; the quake had shaken landslips across the road.

Just over on the right-hand side was a pull-off. I recognized it, and parked, and walked down a familiar track.

The yeasty smell of leaves and brushwood rose about me as the morning sun steamed moisture out of the rain-damp earth. As I went down into the greenness the broad-leaved trees fell away and I stepped into a nave of redwood trees, towering on either side – aisles and aisles of redwoods which stretched their tall brown tapering piers two hundred feet into the sky until they vanished into vaulting ribs and arches of greenery. Between the trees and leaves shone traceries of light which illuminated my path into the forest.

This was what I had come for; this was the only place to find it. I was standing among the first trees, which once had been in sole dominion, and had cleansed the acid-poisoned atmosphere of the planet so that animal life could begin. When we are among them we share the apprehensions of the very earliest men, who knew nothing but forest; it is their sense of awe and majesty that stirs in our brains. Nowhere on earth is more silent or more holy. Their music is the Sanctus of Beethoven's *Missa Solemnis* – great dark valleys of the soul through which soars the violin like a solitary angel lifting its wingtips to the light. *Benedictus qui venit in nomine domini. Hosanna in excelsis.*

I clambered between two trees and came out above the steep rocky descent into the Garden of Eden. Framed in branches of dripping yellow blossom, the curve of white sand spilled peacefully into the embrace of the San Lorenzo River, as it slowed on its journey and shallowed into a wide pool of bright water. I stopped where I was for a moment. At last I had found something which was unchanging, exactly as I remembered it.

Suddenly a shrieking whistle and hiss of air shattered the peacefulness. I sprang up. Through the trees, just the other side of the San Lorenzo River, burst a great snaking monster garbed in orange and purple and brown. With a whoosh and an iron slam of wheels on new-laid track, an old-fashioned, cone-funnelled, cowcatcher steam engine clattered by, carrying a horde of fun-seekers in shorts and T-shirts down towards the Santa Cruz beachfront.

Did any of the younger ones glance backward? They

Christopher Hudson

might have briefly glimpsed, between the trees, across the river, a grown-up Englishman in long trousers whooping and waving his arms in the air. They might have nodded and grinned; they might even have saluted him back.

I didn't go down into the Garden of Eden. It was enough to know that I hadn't imagined it. I walked back through the church of redwoods and out to the main road.